The
ABCs
of Homeschooling

The
ABCs
of Homeschooling

VICKI CARUANA

CROSSWAY BOOKS • WHEATON, ILLINOIS
A DIVISION OF GOOD NEWS PUBLISHERS

The ABCs of Homeschooling

Copyright © 2001 by Vicki Caruana

Published by Crossway Books
      A division of Good News Publishers
      1300 Crescent Street
      Wheaton, Illinois 60187

Cover design: Liita Forsyth

Cover illustration: The Image Bank

Scripture quotations marked NIV are taken from the *Holy Bible: New International Version*®. Copyright © 1973, 1978, 1984 by International Bible Society. Used by permission of Zondervan Publishing House. All rights reserved. The "NIV" and "New International Version" trademarks are registered in the United States Patent and Trademark Office by International Bible Society. Use of either trademark requires the permission of International Bible Society.

Scripture quotations marked ASV are taken from the *American Standard Version.*

Scripture quotations marked KJV are taken from the King James Version.

Scripture quotations marked NLT are taken from *New Living Translation.* Copyright © 1996 by Tyndale House Publishers, Wheaton, Illinois 60187.

First printing, 2001

Printed in the United States of America

The author is represented by Alive Communications, Inc., 7680 Goddard Street, Suite 200, Colorado Springs, CO 80920.

Library of Congress Cataloging-in-Publication Data
Caruana, Vicki.
   The ABCs of homeschooling / Vicki Caruana.
      p.   cm.
   Includes bibliographical references and index.
   ISBN 1-58134-258-6 (trade pbk. : alk. paper)
    1. Homeschooling.   I. Title: ABCs of homeschooling.   II. Title.
LC40.C375   2001
371.04'2—dc21   2001000477
                                               CIP

15	14	13	12	11	10	09	08	07	06	05	04	03	02	01
15	14	13	12	11	10	9	8	7	6	5	4	3	2	1

This book is dedicated to my husband, Chip,
and my sons, Christopher and Charles,

who hold me accountable for everything I've written
in this book!

Table of Contents

Acknowledgments

I would like to thank my agent, Chip MacGregor of Alive Communications, who believes in my ability to communicate even when I have strangling doubts.

I would also like to thank Marvin Padgett and all those at Crossway Books who believed in the message of this book enough to give it life.

Introduction

It seems that everyone today knows someone who homeschools. Even if only by acquaintance in the grocery store, parents are faced with the prospect of homeschooling. Just a brief encounter with a homeschooler sparks debate, discussion, and at times decision. It is no longer easily dismissed as a fringe movement. It is mainstream America.

Choosing to homeschool for some is an easy decision. For others it can be an excruciating process, one through which they go kicking and screaming! This book speaks to all homeschoolers, past, present, and future. Even those who raise their eyebrows unapprovingly at the mother in the grocery store with her school-age children at 11 A.M. can benefit from many of the issues discussed in this book. As you seek information about homeschooling through this book, you may decide that homeschooling is not for you. Guess what? That's okay. This book has no guilt-instilling power! I believe that the Holy Spirit needs no help from me with regard to directing someone else's life.

The choice to homeschool can be broken down into three manageable categories: "Assumptions and Attitudes," "The Basics," and "Character and Cooperation." The first part challenges what you assume to be true, your beliefs and your attitude toward education. The second part provides basic practical information with regard to getting started. Finally, the third part gives you a glimpse into what you can hope to gain from homeschooling and how you can give back. Each chapter gives you a chance for personal reflection and discovery about your own particular situation. Take the time to look inside your own motives and character.

My goal is to give you enough information to make an enlightened decision. Even if you yourself do not choose to homeschool, you'll never look at homeschooling quite the same again. This way we can approach one another with tolerance, wisdom, and love!

PART I

ATTITUDES AND ASSUMPTIONS

Is Homeschooling
Right for Your Family?

BEFORE I HAD CHILDREN, I had a set of preconceived notions of what that would be like. I expected certain things to happen in a certain order. I expected to have three children, a mixture of boys and girls who were no more than two years apart. I expected to be a stay-at-home mom until they went to school. That leads me to my final expectation—that they *would* eventually go to school. Even when our two boys were toddlers (I never had that baby girl), the other mothers in our play group and I would envision the day when our children would be in school and we could finally finish a cup of coffee together uninterrupted!

During that time that same group of women had differing ideas of where and if their children would go to school. We all went to the same church and had known each other since our children were born. We had similar interests and firmly held the same beliefs. Yet when the discussion of school choice came up, it always divided us, and at times I felt like the outsider. You see, I was the only one choosing to send our children to public school.

What I have learned, however, is to expect the unexpected, never say never, and realize that nothing is written in stone (except God's Word). My husband and I now homeschool, and the choice that was furthest from my mind years ago has become the sweetest expression of my commitment to our children that I can imagine. Never say never! Circumstances change, people change, and hearts change. God laughs when we unequivocally make decisions using words like *always, forever*, and *never*. God is the one with the plan. It's a matter of us being a part of His will, not Him being a part of ours. What is His will for *your* family?

I will not tell you there is only one right way to educate a child. There isn't. I am grateful that options are available for parents to choose what is right for the needs of their particular children. Throughout this book you will hear the stories of why other families have chosen to homeschool their children. Some always knew; others didn't make this choice until their children were in secondary school. The reasons are as diverse as the families themselves. And that's the beauty of it all.

As a Christian, it isn't a matter of "finding your own way"; it's a matter of finding God's way. He points out that path through His Word, through circumstances, and through people He has placed in your lives. Be open. Be willing to hear what others have to say. If you are sticking close to the Bible, you will be able to discern truth when you hear it. That assurance is another way the Holy Spirit prods us. It took at least three years of the prodding (a continual tapping on my shoulder, which I defiantly shooed away) of the Holy Spirit before I was obedient and brought our children home. I don't know what God's will is for your family, but I am confident that He will tell you—if you are willing to hear Him.

WHAT DOES GOD'S WORD SAY ABOUT SCHOOLING?

The Bible speaks about training a child in the way he should go (Proverbs 22:6). That is a direct command to parents to train or teach their children in the ways of the Lord. Many adhere to this verse as a call to homeschooling by all Christians. Others cling to it as a parent's ultimate duty no matter what the school setting. If your goal is to lead your children to Christ and then train them to serve Him, you will have to decide in which environment that can best be accomplished. For a long time I believed I could send my children to public school and provide them with enough training at home in spiritual matters. I tried for three years to accomplish this.

However, time just didn't allow it. After-school hours were filled with homework, lessons, clubs, and sports. Precious little time was left over. I looked to our church to train them as well, but at that time our church's youth ministries left a lot to be desired. I think God used that lack to show me that it wasn't up to the church to train my children—it was up to me.

Some Christians choose Christian schools for this very reason. During the day, students attend chapel and are taught with Christian curriculum and have a Bible class to top it all off. Somehow, though, they are just as busy after school as their public school counterparts, and there is still little time for parents to train their children. Leaving it all up to the school is not only foolish but is bound to disappoint you.

The Bible says much about who should teach your children, whether official teachers, parents, role models, or peers. Children are disciples to be led and taught. They will be like their teachers. Whoever your children spend time with will teach them. What do you want them to learn, and whom do you want to teach them? Choose carefully. It is your job to ensure that everyone who teaches them does so to the glory of God. Can you say that from where you sit now? Or do you have to switch places in order to establish that success?

How Do You Know If God Wants You to Homeschool?

God wants you to know His will for you and for your children's lives. Paul used this term many times as he wrote to the churches. God sent Paul and the other apostles so that people would not remain ignorant. He left us His Word so we would know all He wanted us to know. God reveals His will to us in a variety of ways.

He reveals it through His Word. God's Word is sufficient for all things and applies to every situation in life.

> *But you must remain faithful to the things you have been taught. You know they are true, for you know you can trust those who*

*taught you. You have been taught the holy Scriptures from child-
hood, and they have given you the wisdom to receive the salvation
that comes by trusting in Christ Jesus. All Scripture is inspired by
God and is useful to teach us what is true and to make us realize
what is wrong in our lives. It straightens us out and teaches us to
do what is right. It is God's way of preparing us in every way, fully
equipped for every good thing God wants us to do.*

—2 TIMOTHY 3:14-17 (NLT)

The Bible teaches us what to do to bring glory to God. It will never lead us astray. But in order for us to know what it says about our lives, we must be in the Word, studying it on our own.

He reveals His will through action or inaction. Answer to prayer is something we all seek. If we pray for His will to be done in our lives, we can be sure it will be. God is faithful to hear our prayers if we are faithful. If you desire to please and glorify Him in all that you say and do, He will direct your path. Things may happen or not happen that point the way. Circumstances may change, guiding you in a different direction. There's nothing mystical or mysterious about this. If you are truly seeking His way, then welcome everything that happens as a part of His will for you. That may mean you'll run into countless obstacles that seem to scream at you to turn back. That may mean doors will open that you could never have opened on your own, ushering you forward. Or nothing may change, and you are asked to stay the course.

He reveals His will through people. The people in our lives, whether family, friends, acquaintances, or even speakers and writers, are not there by chance. God does everything with purpose and deliberateness, seeking to glorify Himself. This book may be in your hands now by the prodding of the Holy Spirit. The attitudes and opinions of like-minded people should not be undervalued. What matters is, what is your mind like? Do you strive to have the mind of Christ (1 Corinthians 2:16)? If so, surround yourself with others who desire the same, and then you can trust their counsel. Beware, however, of being perpetually surrounded with the opinions of those who are not of the same mind. Their counsel will confuse and trouble you. And God is not the author of "confusion" (1 Corinthians 14:33, ASV).

If you seek His will for your life and for the lives of your children, you will find it.

IS HOMESCHOOLING FOR EVERYONE?

I have worked with too many children, both in schools and out of them, to believe there is only one right way to teach anyone. With that in mind I do not believe homeschooling is for every family, or for that matter for every child in every family. Individual needs of children must be taken into account. Many choose to homeschool because their child has special needs that are not being met in a traditional school setting. Others realize that in order for their child's morality to reflect their parents', they need to come home to school. And still others know that the best way to re-instill a lost love for learning is to reignite that fire at home. Whatever the need, homeschooling can fill it. Can the public or private school make that same claim? Can curriculum be tailored to the level of each child in a school? No. Children will fail; whether or not it is their fault is at question.

A "special needs" child may not be one who has already been so labeled by the school system. It may be a child who at seven is still not reading. Cause for concern? Not necessarily. Especially when all educational research shows that children are developmentally ready to learn to read anywhere between four and eight years old. So what's the rush? Earlier in their lives we found out that it wasn't effective to rush them through potty training. So why is it okay to rush them through school? Knowing your child's developmental level and acting accordingly will promote peace in your home and instill confidence in a young child.

With the atrocities recently committed on school campuses, it is no wonder parents of secondary schoolchildren are opting out. A sense of morality and absolute truth can no longer be found. Everyone is permitted to believe whatever is true for them, we are told. So if two teenage boys in Colorado believe they have the right to kill their classmates, that's truth for them? Nonsense! What truth do you want *your* children to be surrounded by? If it is God's truth, consider where that truth will be propagated.

Some children have lost interest in school altogether, either because they have experienced failure too often too early in their young academic lives, or because they are very bright but have never been challenged enough to care. Both need attention. The love for learning in many children, perhaps even yours, is gone. Whether it is temporary or permanent is up to you. What will you do about it? Lack of motivation is the number one killer of achievement in students. As their parent, you are also their best advocate. Find out what they need, and give it to them. You may find that you are the only one who can.

ARE THERE REASONS *NOT* TO HOMESCHOOL?

Many homeschooling proponents do not believe there are reasons not to homeschool, only excuses. I disagree. There are many parents who desire to homeschool, yet cannot because of a debilitating illness, loss of revenue that causes both parents to work outside the home, and single parents who are unable to stay at home with their children. I sympathize with these families. Yet my question, already raised by Gregg Harris in his book *The Christian Home School*, is, "Where is the church?" If a parent desires to be obedient by homeschooling, the church should offer support. However, if these reasons are instead excuses, the person doesn't really want to homeschool in the first place. It is just a matter of being honest with oneself.

There is another reason that may be the only one I would say is a good reason: Your spouse does not want you to homeschool. In a two-parent family, both parents must agree that homeschooling is the right choice for their children. It is a matter of submitting to one another (Ephesians 5:21) in order to have peace. If the matter causes strife, that tension is not of God. This situation may simply be due to a lack of information or understanding. If your partner doesn't really know any homeschoolers or the advantages of this option, try to educate him or her. But don't nag. My husband was unsure until we went together to our state homeschooling convention. There he witnessed thousands of fathers carrying little ones on their shoulders and attending a variety of workshops designed just for them. He came away from that convention confident that homeschooling is a good choice.

Is There a "Point of No Return" with This Decision?

There is no contract to sign (unless you count your letter of intent) and no one to tell you that you are too late to start or stop. Your child is never too old to start. As mentioned earlier, more and more parents are pulling their children out of middle and high schools every day. Beginning homeschooling is challenging for parents and children alike, but not impossible. The other end of the spectrum is: If you begin homeschooling, are you locked in, or can you stop? Of course you can stop, but the consensus is that you should finish one full year before deciding whether or not to continue. The first year, no matter what the age of your children, is full of bumps along the way. There are plenty of days when you will want to quit and will catch yourself thinking, *If you guys don't shape up, I'm sending you back to school!*

I believe in taking it a year at a time. Other proponents say you should plan to go the distance no matter what and graduate your children from homeschool, but that may not be realistic for many. Even if you only do it for a short time, homeschooling is beneficial.

Am I Qualified to Teach My Children?

It wasn't until recent history that the education of children was delegated to an institution. Parents have traditionally taught their own children. It's not the parents' ability to teach that has changed. We are more educated than any of our forefathers were. And you know your child better than any teacher ever could. You will do whatever it takes to provide him or her with the best education. After all, you know what he or she needs. You also know when he or she is too tired or too sick or too distracted to work properly. You know what motivates him or her, and you know what doesn't. You also love him or her and have a bigger stake in his success than a teacher does. You have the advantage of natural "looping." (Looping is a term used to describe a group of students having the same teacher at least two years in a row by design.) Looping is something many teachers want because they get to have their students for two years in a row. They know continuity fosters success in the classroom. As a homeschool parent you can "loop" for as long as you want!

You are already your child's best teacher. You taught him how to walk, how to speak, how to eat, how to play alone and with others. You taught him how to trust, how to love, and ultimately how to follow the Lord. What more proof do you need? You are qualified simply because you are his parent and want the best for him. You can have peaceful assurance that you can teach him.

🍎 PAULINE

"You're going to do what?" I exclaimed at my best friend as she looked at me sheepishly.

"I'm going to homeschool Greg and Emily." She paused. "Tom and I have talked it over and feel that's the best way to educate them. I've also been impressed by other homeschoolers I've met."

I couldn't believe it. Joanne lived right around the corner. Our kids were the same age. I was planning on carpooling with them, and maybe Joanne would have time to spend with just me. Not changing diapers, not settling squabbles, not cleaning messes. Besides that, I had just started freelance writing and was looking forward to concentrating on a book.

But the bug had hit . . .

I started questioning other homeschool moms. I started imagining what it would be like to have my kids home all day teaching them. I started thinking how it would benefit our family since my husband worked each weekend and barely saw the children while they were at school. But most importantly, God started to speak to me. Not audibly, of course. It was really just a sense that God was saying, "If I wanted you to homeschool, would you?" And so it went. Finally the decision was made. I would teach them at home.

So when people asked me why I decided to homeschool, I said something like, "Because God said so."

When I started, I was scared. I could direct a musical, sing or speak in public, write an article. But could I teach my children? I remember the first day. My three-year-old and my first-grader were standing there looking at me expectantly as I held the flag and we said the Pledge of Allegiance. I cried.

I've cried a lot over the last five years. Sometimes out of frustration, sometimes out of anger, oftentimes out of joy. I've laughed a lot too. Like the time we were studying trees. We went to a restaurant that had a huge camphor tree, maybe 300 years old. I brought a small stepladder since the plan was to study trees in a tree. We had breakfast and trekked out to the tree. I tried stepping up to it. I tried jumping up into it. My kids even tried to boost me up into it. It was no use. Finally we decided to ask someone to help us. We strategically placed ourselves at the entrance to the restaurant where we looked for just the right person. A nice family of four arrived. I approached them with a casual explanation that we homeschooled and were studying trees and I needed a boost. They were very receptive until the part about the boost. The father declined after receiving a life-threatening glare from his wife.

Not only have I cried and laughed a lot, but I've reflected a lot.

One day my daughter had just physically become a woman, and we decided to take a personal day, just the two of us. We had a leisurely breakfast at the beach and decided to take a long walk. As we were walking side by side, only glancing at each other occasionally, she asked me some very personal questions about my life, my involvement with boys, and my beliefs. We were definitely at level five communication. I thought about that a lot—how we could just take a day off in the middle of the week to be together and really talk. The five years I spent homeschooling would have been worth it for just that one day.

Homeschooling has also humbled me and continues to humble me. I know I can't do it alone. Each time I try, I fall flat on my face. This year has been an especially hard one for me. I don't know why. A veteran homeschool mom once told me that the fifth or sixth year tends to be the hardest; so maybe the worst is over. My daughter wanted to go to school. "Nothing personal—I just want to go," she said. My mind said, *Let her go—you're doing a rotten job. She'd be better off with someone else.* But my heart kept saying *No!* In desperation I prayed, *Lord, if You want her to stay home, change her mind.* In the meantime, I told her I wasn't sending her to school unless God told me to. After all, He had been the one to tell me to start in the first place. A couple of weeks later she had found a couple of new homeschool friends and spoke about homeschooling next year. So for at least a year, I'm doing it again.

"Why?" you might ask. Because I like being with my children. Because our family likes each other. But most important, because God said so. That's good enough for me.

Is homeschooling right for your family? Only you can answer that. Run every excuse—I mean reason—through the Word of God. Follow His leading by watching for actions and circumstances that reveal a path. And listen for truth in the counsel of others. Pray for wisdom, and God will give it (Proverbs 2:1-6).

ADVANTAGES OF HOMESCHOOLING

1. Homeschooling allows parents to meet the individual learning needs of their children.

2. Homeschooling ensures that the parents' morals, values, and beliefs will be passed on.

3. Homeschooling offers multiage learning.

4. Homeschooling offers the continuity of the same teacher year after year.

5. Homeschooling offers time for apprenticeship opportunities.

6. Homeschooling gives fathers who work long or odd hours a chance to be with their children.

7. Homeschooling costs less.

8. Homeschooling helps family members grow closer to one another.

9. Homeschooling fosters independent learning.

10. Homeschooled children score at or above their peers on standardized tests.

11. Homeschooled children learn cooperative work habits earlier and more efficiently.

12. Homeschooling provides children with opportunities to study topics in depth.

FOR MORE INFORMATION ON THIS TOPIC

The Christian Home School by Gregg Harris (Wolgemuth & Hyatt, 1988).

Warning: Nonsense Is Destroying America by Vincent Ryan Ruggiero (Thomas Nelson, 1994).

The Homeschooling Book of Answers by Linda Dobson (Prima, 1998).

COUNT THE COST/REAP THE JOY

1. What intrigues you about homeschooling?

_____

_____

_____

2. If you struggle with this issue, finish this sentence(s). Choose whichever applies best.

I could never homeschool because

_____

_____

_____

I don't think homeschooling is for us because

_____

_____

_____

I'd like to homeschool, but

_____

_____

_____

3. Have you talked to your spouse about homeschooling? What does he or she think?

_____

_____

_____

4. Below write what you believe the philosophy or purpose of education is. (You will revisit this statement later in the book.)

_____

_____

_____

5. Begin a fact-finding mission. If you know homeschoolers, invite them over and talk to them. Read more about homeschooling. And most of all, PRAY!

Why Homeschool? I

*Belief: God has ordained homeschooling
as a Christian parent's calling.*

*And these words, which I command thee this day, shall be upon
thy heart, and thou shalt teach them diligently unto thy children,
and shalt talk of them when thou sittest in thy house, and when
thou walkest by the way, and when thou liest down, and when
thou risest up.*

—DEUTERONOMY 6:6-7 (ASV)

This particular verse is considered a call to homeschooling for
many Christian parents. It is a very powerful call, one that has
changed the lives of many parents and children. This verse has provided a framework within which parents can educate their children.
It tells us what to teach, how to teach, where to teach, and when to
teach. It appears all-encompassing.

WHAT TO TEACH

*"And these words, which I command thee this day, shall be upon
thy heart."*

"These words" refers to God's commandments, precepts, and
statutes. Parents are expected to be the ones to educate their children in God's ways. This is expected no matter what type of schooling your child receives—public, private, or home. But many parents

believe that the only way they can be obedient to God in this matter is to bring their children home to school. And they may be right.

Janice wasn't sure she could handle all the academics her seventh grader required, but she was sure his spiritual growth depended greatly upon how well she taught him God's laws and God's ways. Despite eight years in a Christian school, a good teaching church, and a dynamic youth group, she saw her son slipping away spiritually. Her friends told her that she pulled him out of school out of desperation, and they were probably right. Janice was afraid that if she didn't act right then, she might lose her son forever.

Admittedly, many Christians will not even consider sending their children to public or private school, because they are afraid of what will happen to them there. However, we are not called to fear but can have the assurance that God has already overcome the world! Whether you choose to keep your children with you out of an overwhelming fear or from an overwhelming sense that it is your number one job to teach them God's Word and ways, you are still left with the question of what to teach them.

God's Word is the foundation upon which every other subject is built. Everything, from spelling to science, needs to be sifted through His Word. Every subject, every man-made principle, must be measured by His law, His principles, and His promises. So when you look at this verse and read "these words," you need to first be clear of what they are, and, second, must know how to communicate them to your children.

How to Teach

"And thou shalt teach them diligently unto thy children."

To me this verse is the bottom line. How do you teach with diligence? According to *Vine's Bible Dictionary*, when you teach diligently, you teach in earnest and carefully. It's not something you wait around to do. Time is short. Our children are only on loan to us from the Father. It is with utmost earnestness that we teach them the ways of the Lord. But we are also to do it with care. It is a deliberate act, one that is carefully planned and executed. It is not done haphazardly or without purpose.

There is a homeschool philosophy called unschooling that puts the learner in charge of his (or her) own learning. The child is led by his interests, talents, and strengths. Curriculum choices are explored and rejected based upon whether or not they fit the child, and not the other way around. The underlying premise is that since no two children are alike, there is no one right way to teach all children. This is true. However, even an unschooling approach must use God's Word as its basic curriculum. His truth should lead the child, not the other way around. If you are teaching your child that God is faithful, that He is a God of order and purpose and is sovereign, how you homeschool should reflect those beliefs.

The opposites of diligence are lethargy and sloth. Proverbs is full of reasons why we should avoid those last two particular traits. So if you desire to obey Deuteronomy 6:6-7, you must teach your children His ways in earnest and carefully—"diligently." And that is a full-time job!

WHEN AND WHERE TO TEACH

> ". . . and shalt talk of them when thou sittest in thy house, and when thou walkest by the way, and when thou liest down, and when thou risest up."

Look how globally this verse describes when and where we should teach our children about God and His commandments. Sometimes when our children go to a traditional school, opportunities like the ones described above come few and far between. Mornings are so hectic as we get them awake, fed, and off to school that thoughts of devoting time to God "when thou risest up" never enter our mind. We just hope we remembered to pack their lunches and gym clothes! The passage in Deuteronomy is a command, and it takes more than bedtime prayers to fulfill it. It requires a great deal of one-on-one time.

The great debate of quality versus quantity time still rages on today. Working parents, feeling guilty about how much time they spend away from their children, are convinced that all they need to do is spend a little quality time with their children, and all will be well. God's Word advocates both quality and quantity time in these verses. For many of us the only way we can obey God's Word on this point is to bring our children home. We need more, not less time with them. It's like making a hearty loaf of bread. If you put it in the fire to bake before it has had a chance to rise, it will fall flat. Our children need more time than we have been giving them if we are to prepare them for the life God intends for them.

You may well be able to balance your time so well that on the way to soccer practice or before bedtime you capture teachable moments to really minister to your children and to teach them what it means to be a child of God. But some of us know we can't. Some of us already know we aren't doing a good enough job of obeying this verse. Some of us need to bring our children home in order to do it God's way.

Caution: The Word of God should never be taken out of context. For example, in this verse you can easily misunderstand what "teach them" refers to. "Them" does not refer to children. It refers to God's laws, statutes, and principles. If you read the entire chapter, you see that clearly. If you are going to use God's Word to justify your actions, you must be a diligent (there's that word again) student of it as well as a good steward of it.

WHAT IT SAYS BEFORE THIS VERSE

Prior to this verse, we read:

> *"These are the commands, decrees and laws the LORD your God directed me to teach you to observe in the land that you are crossing the Jordan to possess, so that you, your children and their chil-*

dren after them may fear the LORD your God as long as you live by keeping all his decrees and commands that I give you, and so that you may enjoy long life. Hear, O Israel, and be careful to obey so that it may go well with you and that you may increase greatly in a land flowing with milk and honey, just as the LORD, the God of your fathers, promised you. Hear, O Israel: The LORD our God, the LORD is one. Love the LORD your God with all your heart and with all your soul and with all your strength."

—DEUTERONOMY 6:1-5 (NIV)

As you can see, "teach them" refers to God's "commands, decrees and laws." You can also see that academics are secondary to this commandment—they are not even mentioned. But if you believe the only way you can obey this command is to bring your children home, then according to the world's standards you are also responsible for their academic education.

WHAT IT SAYS AFTER THIS VERSE

We must remember to keep this verse in context. The verses that follow Deuteronomy 6:6-7 (verses 8-25) tell why it is important to obey these words. Here is part of that section:

"Tie them as symbols on your hands and bind them on your fore-heads. Write them on the doorframes of your houses and on your gates."

—VERSES 8-9 (NIV)

The people used these deliberate acts to memorize and keep before them God's law. It is just as important today to memorize Scripture. If you are to obey God's law, you must first know it. Yes, if your child goes to a private Christian school he is probably learning verses every week. Yes, if he is going to a youth group that memorizes Scripture, he is learning verses. But can he apply what he has learned to everyday situations? Can he communicate to you his understanding when he sits, when he walks, when he lies down, and when he rises up? If this doesn't characterize your home, you have some changes to make.

CAN YOU OBEY THIS SCRIPTURE IF YOU DON'T HOMESCHOOL?

Our obedience to God is not dependent upon circumstances. Our own will is weak, and that is the real problem. But if we are walking in the Spirit, we will be able to recognize situations and circumstances that lead to God and those that don't. The real question is not, *can* you obey? but, *will* you obey? You will have peace when you are walking within His will. Do you have peace about where your child goes to school? If so, thank Him now for that peace. If you don't, ask Him for wisdom.

IS IT A SIN IF YOU ARE A CHRISTIAN AND DO NOT HOMESCHOOL?

God did not say in His Word, "Thou shalt not send your children to public school!" However, if you believe that God has led you and your children out of the public or private school, then for you it is sin. In Romans 14 Paul expounds on the liberties we have in Christ. As long as our pursuits do not lead others into sin, we should feel free to engage in them. We have a tendency to harshly judge other ways to worship, other ways to spend our free time, and other ways to educate our children. If you are content with your choice of schooling at this point, don't feel guilty for not homeschooling. On the other hand, if you are not content with where your children go to school, don't keep them there out of fear of what others will say. Paul goes on to say, "So whatever you believe about these things keep between yourself and God. Blessed is the man who does not condemn himself by what he approves" (verse 22, NIV). This choice is between you and the Lord.

   I can still remember how I felt years ago when our children were attending public school. Very few parents at our church sent their children to public school. Even though at the time I felt that the boys were where God wanted them, I couldn't help wondering if I was doing something wrong. It was a struggle to keep it between myself and God. Everyone had an opinion about it, and some didn't hesitate to let me know. Now that we homeschool, believe it or not, there are still many people out there willing to give us an earful of what they think about our choice. But this verse is clear. If you approve of where you've chosen to send your children to school, do not condemn yourself for making that choice. If, however, you do not approve of your current choice, it is a sin for you to remain there. Again, this is between you and God.

YOUR CHILD, YOUR CHOICE

On the surface it may seem as if you are actually making this choice out of your own will. But if you are a Christian, the Holy Spirit lives inside you and guides you in your choices. Are you striving to hear Him? We are all accountable before God for our choices, including where we choose to send our children to school. What we must remember is, who is leading us toward this choice? Some who choose homeschooling may be doing it out of God's will. Whatever you choose, make sure it is within God's will for your family. Pray specifically for wisdom, watch and listen for the Holy Spirit's leading, and then make your choice with full confidence in God's sovereignty.

BETH

I first heard of homeschooling in the fall of 1981 when I heard a Focus on the Family radio program—Dr. Dobson interviewing Dr. Raymond Moore about his brand-new book *Home Grown Kids*. At that time my son was two years old, and I was pregnant with my daughter. My husband and I were planning to go to the mission field; so I didn't thinking homeschooling in the States would ever affect me, but I did think it sounded like a good idea. I planned to teach my children on the mission field using correspondence courses, as my mother had taught me for first grade. But

I planned to do it longer than she had—how long would depend on what kind of personalities my kids would have.

As it turned out, the Lord closed the door to the mission field; so I decided that I would homeschool. At first I really only planned to do so for my son's kindergarten year, using the first grade curriculum I had prepared while I was in college majoring in elementary education. We'd see how it went.

It went well, especially considering I knew no other homeschoolers in the area, or even that there were any, until near the end of that school year. Our son learned really well. So by the end of his kindergarten year I felt he would be bored if he went into a regular classroom where the kids need to stay together. So we decided to continue on with homeschooling him, at least until our daughter started homeschooling. He would be entering third grade when she began kindergarten.

To make a long story short, God blessed our homeschooling efforts, and we continued through to the end. We did choose to send our son to a Christian school for his last year of high school, but that in itself was part of his "hands-on" education. He thought he wanted to be a high school teacher, and we figured it would be good for him to see what high school was like since he had never been to regular school at all. We didn't want him to go through four years of college, get into the classroom, and find he hated it! Our daughter did not have this need; so we homeschooled her through twelfth grade, from which she just graduated.

I am glad to have finished homeschooling because I see that God used it to develop our children into godly adults. I don't take credit for that, believe me! God did it in spite of my imperfections. But I do know that He chose to use homeschooling to do this. I'd do it over again. I have no regrets.

FOR MORE INFORMATION ON THIS TOPIC

Homeschooling for Excellence by David and Micki Colfax (Warner Books, 1988).

Success in School: Building on Biblical Principles by Vicki Caruana (Focus Publishing, Bemidji, Minnesota, 2000).

The Christian Home School by Gregg Harris (Noble Publishing, 1995).

The Home Schooling Father by Michael P. Farris (Loyal Publishing, 1999).

Count the Cost/Reap the Joy

Even homeschoolers who initially made this choice for academic or safety reasons are reminded by the Holy Spirit about the spiritual reasons. God shows me daily why my children are home with me. We wouldn't have time otherwise to teach them God's laws, principles, and ways. I left the Super Mom complex behind years ago! Whether you choose to homeschool or not, Deuteronomy 6 still applies. Ponder this passage (especially verses 6-7) and look at your life. Then answer the following questions.

1. After reading this chapter, my reaction to Deuteronomy 6 is:

_____

_____

_____

2. List ways in which *you* are currently teaching God's laws, principles, and ways to your children.

_____

_____

_____

3. God wants us to spend both *quality* and *quantity* time in His Word. Which do you need to improve in order to effectively communicate His Word to your children? How will you do that?

_____

_____

_____

4. Evaluate if your current choice of schooling meets the expectations of Deuteronomy 6:6-7. Pray about it right now.

Why Homeschool? II

Belief: Values should be transmitted by family members, not schools.

"MOM . . ." DANNY HESITATES. "Will you homeschool me next year?"

The words jump from Linda's mouth before she has time to think about them. "No. Absolutely not!" After all, he's in seventh grade, and she has a life!

Weeks go by, and Danny asks again and again, "Mom, please homeschool me." Finally Linda is at her wit's end. "Why?" she asks, exasperated.

For the first time in weeks, Danny is quiet. His eyes are glued to the floor. *What is the problem?* Linda wonders. And then it hits her. "Has something happened at school? What is it? Tell me!" Protective instincts spark to life, and Linda's eyes are wide as she waits for her son to answer.

"Nothing . . . Well, nothing that terrible," Danny begins. "It's just that I feel out of place."

"Everyone feels out of place now and then, hon. It's part of growing up." Linda is sure her son's words won't be enough to make her change her mind.

"No one believes what we believe. I just don't think I belong there." Danny's eyes are desperate now.

"Is there anything else?" Linda hopes there isn't.

"Well, I'd like to work ahead, but they don't let you. They've even cut the summer work-ahead classes. So I'm stuck." Danny hopes this truthful yet more practical approach will help her understand how serious he is.

Linda gives her usual honest but almost pat answer. "I'll think about it and pray about it. Don't ask me again. Give me some time."

Danny's eyes light up with hope. Maybe, just maybe she'll see how important this is to him.

Linda and Danny's situation is far from unusual. I know it may be hard to believe, but many young people beg their parents to homeschool them. It may be the very reason *you* are reading this book. The two reasons cited in the above scenario are both valid reasons to choose homeschooling for your children, no matter how old they are. What is sad is that sometimes we weigh more heavily the practical over the moral reasons presented. (How important is where and from whom our children obtain their values?) Is it important enough to bring them home? What are the dangers associated with keeping our children in school, public or private? And finally, if we do bring them home to school, what are our character goals for them?

WHERE DO OUR VALUES COME FROM?

As a Christian parent, you have one choice and only one choice as to where your values should originate. The Bible should be the authority in your life. Where you spend your time and with whom will show your children what you value, what your priorities are. On what do you spend your money? Who are your heroes? We must ask ourselves these questions before we can effectively guide our children in clarifying those same values for themselves.

Time Well Spent

What is most important to you in your life tends to be that on which you spend the most time. It is a matter of priorities. Your children may be at school all day, and you are so happy to be running your day your way! It's a milestone. The world applauds, and you breathe a sigh of relief. Or you may still have preschool-age children at home, and your time is not your own at all. Practical day-to-day living consumes you, and you fall into bed exhausted each night. Even those who already homeschool wrestle with how they spend their time. You may still find yourself spending more time in your car than with your kids. Interestingly, none of these scenarios is unusual. In fact, they are all expected and accepted ways to spend your time. But God wants more for His children.

When all of your children are finally in school, you may volunteer for ministries that you've waited years to do. You may even take on leadership roles that your schedule just didn't allow before. Indeed, God wants you to spend time with and for Him. However, many tend to become too busy doing God's work and forget the needs of their families (probably the most important part of His work for them). They never plan it that way—it just happens. But that's the problem. They didn't have a plan for how they would spend their time once their children were in school full-time. Keep in mind that you are still responsible to teach your child to love and serve the Lord. That is the priority. All your busyness teaches them is that busyness is what is expected. Is that what you intended them to learn? Ask yourself today what your children are learning from you and how you spend your days.

Parents at home with preschoolers are the most tired people around. Such a life is physically as well as emotionally exhausting. I once tried to encourage my sister, whose children were all under three, that things would get better, that there's light at the end of the tunnel. Her response? "I'm just worried it's an oncoming train!" Pretty witty for such a tired person. It's hard to see and hear God amidst temper tantrums and piles of laundry, but you can. After all, He has overcome the world; so I doubt that a pile of dirty diapers could get in His way! You may have to strain to hear Him, carving out definite slivers of time just to sit and listen. Your prayer time will not only rejuvenate you but can also teach your preschoolers what is most important to you. Convicted of this, one woman forced herself to wake up just fifteen minutes before her sleeping darlings so she could have a quiet time that consisted mostly of prayer. Five minutes into her prayer time she heard the shuffling of little feet at the stairs. Her oldest, only four, wanted to know if she could get up. "No, sweetie. Go back to bed. Mommy is praying." This little girl thought that was wonderful—so wonderful that she wanted to join Mommy! No more quiet time for this woman. It is important that you keep your quiet time *your* quiet time. It's important that our children see how important time alone with God is. What do your children see about your time with God?

Even homeschoolers get caught up in the busyness of life. It's not easy to teach your children, keep house, plan and cook meals, etc. It's a delicate balancing act to say the least. Add to it a myriad of activities, lessons, and programs your children become involved in, and you find yourself rushing around as frantically as you would if they were in a public or Christian school every day! And many times that busyness gives way to even more busyness, and your teaching is pushed aside. What was once a concentrated effort becomes only a fleeting moment in time; school is put on the back burner. Believe it or not, that is still teaching your children something: It teaches them that school is not that important. Is that what you wanted them to learn?

How we spend our time is an indicator of what we value. God wants us to have His values, and God values relationships. His relationship with us is the most important one we can have. How much time do you spend working on that relationship? Our children will learn how to cultivate their own relationship with God by watching us grow ours. Does this mean you may have to make some drastic changes in how you spend your time? Probably. Will bringing your children home to school be one of those necessary changes? Possibly. It will be difficult for them to learn how to love and serve God if they spend more time with others than with you.

Money Well Spent

What we spend our money on is also a strong indicator of what we value. Do you as a family regularly give to God sacrificially? Are your children active participants in this process? Have you shown them how to put away some of their own money for God? Again this takes definite planning; it will not just happen magically. Do your children's friends have the same beliefs about money and how it should be spent? Do their teachers? Those who surround our children will influence their thinking and ultimately their beliefs. What do you want your children to believe?

All that we have is from God—every penny! Becoming a good steward of all that He has provided is time-consuming. It's hard enough as adults to always spend money wisely. This is often a bone of contention between husband and wife, and it has more influence over our decision-making than it should. But where and how you spend your money shows your children what is important to you.

We cannot change how other people raise their children; we can only raise our own. The goal is to raise them to the glory of God. So when they are faced with how their friends spend money, they need a solid foundation to come home to. Schools are poor examples of how to spend money. Fund-raisers have become standard operating practice, and parents are coerced into giving their money to schools when their taxes should have already done that. The goal of a fund-raiser is usually to obtain more materials and/or technology. Bad teaching is not improved with technology, and good teaching doesn't require it. If good teaching depends on state-of-the-art technology, then all teachers prior to the Information Age were lousy—and that is not true. But the idea that money can buy success is prevalent in our schools. We must not let it be so in our homes.

A Hero in the Making

Who are our children's heroes? Up until about age three, Mommy and Daddy are heroes to children. But we're quickly replaced by whatever fad comes along, and then you can see values in action. Whether it's Pokemon®, Power Rangers® or Barbie®, children (and their parents) spend a great deal of time and money to pursue their heroes, even though they are fictional. A hero for a Christian has one purpose—to point us to God and cause us to become more Christlike. The values of heroes are well known. We even know what Superman believes in—truth, justice, and the American way. Teachers used to be heroes, but unfortunately they have been shown to be as flawed as the rest of us. So where do our children look for heroes? If they attend a Christian school, more than likely they will study Christian biographical and biblical figures. If they attend public school, they are studying people from all walks, religions, and lifestyles. Yes, our children should be exposed to different kinds of people and families, but they shouldn't have to accept a sinful lifestyle in order to be politically correct. How about choosing to be your child's hero? It's an important responsibility, but God has already given you the power to be just that for your children.

WHAT IS SECULAR HUMANISM AND WHAT IS IT DOING IN OUR SCHOOLS?

Secular humanism is ingrained in our society as well as in our schools. It subtly proposes that there is no absolute truth, that a person must love himself or herself before he or she can really love anyone else, and that one must accept every lifestyle as appropriate. Everyone's truth is valid, we are told. There is no real evil, just misguided people. As Christian parents we have some major responsibilities. One is to be salt and light in the world. Another is to train our children in the way they should go. This may or may not require homeschooling. It depends upon how well we meet both responsibilities.

God's View vs. the World's View

We are only pilgrims or sojourners in this world. We learn its customs and languages, but since heaven is our real home, we are in a sense not citizens of this world. To be so would mean we would accept and practice all the values attached to this world and leave our heavenly ones behind. We can't base our lives on both.

• The world's eyes look in the mirror for purpose and reason. Ours look above.

• The world believes success is defined by status, money, and self-fulfillment. Our success comes only when we glorify God.

• The world sees learning as a means to better oneself and to become a contributing member of society. God sees learning as a way to become a strong testimony for Him.

All in all, these two views oppose each other. What we believe to be true will show others where or to whom our loyalties lie—a citizen of the world or of heaven. Where do you want your children to reside?

Salt and Light

Christians whose children attend public school believe they and their children will have the opportunity to be salt and light there. This is possible. As an adult, a mature believer, you may be well equipped to be just that in your children's school. And as a representative of heaven, you have the distinct responsibility to protect God's reputation and to point others in His direction. Christian teachers in the public schools have this same mission in mind. The only problem is that our children are not yet mature believers, grounded in the faith, ready to do battle daily.

How does a soldier prepare for battle? Even if his mission is one of search and rescue, he must be carefully trained so he can both protect himself and complete his mission. Are you sure your children are prepared? Some are; some aren't. Hours in public or private schools are not the only times or ways our children can lead other children to the Lord. So much more time is spent in after-school activities and sports. At such times our children can be salt and light with parental supervision. Of course, some children, many of them teens, *are* prepared. Cassie Bernall, a Columbine High School student in Littleton, Colorado, knew what she was standing up against that day in her high school's library. She stood firm for the Gospel, and it cost her her life. Does this mean she shouldn't have been in public school? No. The Gospel was spread, and many kids came to Christ because of her testimony. God's will was fulfilled.

Some of us are called to be witnesses in the public schools. Some are not. God has different jobs for different people at different times. Where does your child belong right now?

TRUTH OR CONSEQUENCES

The argument many parents wage against the teaching of values in the school is "Whose values will they teach? Will those values be in conflict with our own?" Even non-Christians have this concern. What does the Bible say about who we are and how we should behave? What does God think is important? The answers to these questions should clarify matters.

Who Are We?

Maybe you've heard this question before but didn't really understand it. Or maybe you've heard it here for the very first time. The answer is crucial. As Christians:

• We are adopted children of God.
• We are justified through faith.
• We are children of grace (getting what we don't deserve—eternal life).
• We are children of promise.
• We have been given righteousness in Christ. Now when God sees us, He sees His Son.
• We have the power of the Holy Spirit at our disposal.
• We are loved.

We must communicate these truths to our children. So often in school they find out:

• They are not as pretty as others.
• They are not as smart as others.
• They don't belong.
• Different is bad.
• They are alone.
• They don't measure up.
• They are better than others.
• Adults can't be trusted, are stupid, are not like them.
• *Feeling* good is better than *being* good.
• God doesn't exist.

Is that what we send our children to school to learn? No, but often they hear that anyway. You can be the filter that disallows the impurities, but it may take more than volunteering at their school to do that successfully. Everything our children hear, see, and learn must be filtered through the Word of God. What does God say about it? WDGSAI. That's not as catchy as a certain other slogan, I know, but it should always be the question of the day in each of our homes.

Secular humanism is destroying the minds of our children. But God's Word is stronger! You either believe that or you don't. Find out for yourself *what God says about it.*

Choosing to Homeschool for Character Reasons

Many people are becoming convinced that an absence of strong morals is the downfall of our schools, our children, our future. They are right. Without the Bible, all the schools can do is appeal to the conscience. They can give strong suggestions but no truth. They don't know the truth, but you do. Making sure our children know it may be a full-time job. It may mean homeschooling, or it may not. God will let you know. He will confirm it with His Word, wise counsel, and circumstances. Where do your children belong? It depends upon what you want them to learn.

 **DOROTHY**

Homeschooling was not something I had ever imagined I would be doing. I knew of it, heard women talking about it at church, and remembered my sister-in-law homeschooling her two girls when they were young. But it hadn't entered my mind as a possibility for our daughter. I had always assumed that she and I were either too different or maybe too alike to make a peaceful homeschool experience. She is an only child, and I felt that was enough to keep her in school. Besides, I was enjoying my time alone at home working on all the projects I longed to finish.

Then came middle school. Sixth grade started out fine, but by the second semester I noticed a personality change in my daughter. Her grades began to drop—first a little, then a lot. I tried talking to her about it, but she was distant and noncommunicative. Then I tried good old-fashioned threats: "If you don't shape up, I'll pull you out of school and put you in private school!" (I know, I know—a mother's desperation.) When the school year ended and I received her final report card in the mail, my heart dropped in disappointment, discouragement, and bewilderment. Although her average was fine, her last semester had continued the decline. I immediately telephoned the school to speak with any of the teachers involved. But with school out for the summer, there was no one to talk to, no way to find out what went wrong. It's funny how those dead ends tend to bring us to our knees. In seeking God's answer to the problem through prayer, I became keenly aware that my daughter was at a pivotal point in her life. Something told me to act now or suffer the consequences. Something also told me that private school was not the answer for us.

The decision to homeschool would require a sacrifice on my part, but I was hesitant only for a moment. Over the years, through trial and error, I have learned that it is better to be quick to answer God's tug on my heart. Jesus tells us to pick up our cross and follow Him. We are to follow Him into death, burial, and resurrection in every area of our lives. I had to put my own wants to death in order to care for the needs of my daughter's education and character training. But I can be sure that God is faithful to resurrect His plan in both of our lives.

Perhaps the greatest confirmation of God's call to teach my daughter at home came for me when I tried to hug her. I wanted to console her and let her know that my disappointment and frustration in no way negated my love for her. I was not a very huggy type of person; in fact I found hugging uncomfortable and strange. That was something I learned from my father; it was a facet of my personality that I did not like and wanted desperately to change. So I pushed past myself and offered her a hug. To my horror she pushed me away. After the initial shock, I reached for her again, wrapping my arms around her tightly until her fighting finally gave way to tears and limp arms at my side. Over the next few hours she began to confess some problems she had been having in some of her classes and with the character of some of her teachers. The next day I began investigating homeschooling.

Every doubt imaginable crept into my head. *I'm not qualified to teach her.* And, *She's an only child and needs to be around her friends.* But then the obvious seemed to settle in: Who is more qualified than a motivated parent who loves her child? And what's most important about friendship—quantity or quality? I realized that when I was growing up, I didn't have a lot of superficial friends, but rather one or two really good friends. Those friendships were cultivated outside of school. Beyond that, I knew that God does not ask us to do anything without equipping us to do it. If God was in it, I was completely equipped.

Perhaps there was something more I could have been doing in conjunction with the school that would have made things better. But it still would not have been the very best that I could give my daughter. There were also other elements within the school system that had recently come to light, which I had no control over, such as the afternoon my daughter's substitute language arts teacher was arrested and jailed for downloading and printing pornographic material from the Internet while in the classroom! Fortunately one of the students immediately reported the incident to the office.

With prayer and the help of a close friend, we have nearly finished the last lap of our first year of homeschooling. I just received the county-administered standardized test results for my daughter. All of her scores remained in the average and above average range with the exception of spelling and reading comprehension, and those scores have skyrocketed from below average/average to well above average! But much, much more wonderful than that is that my daughter now requests hugs (only when she beats me to it) several times a day! Her attitude has changed significantly, and I can see her delight in acts of godly obedience.

God is not slack in His plan for our lives. He always does much more than we could ever ask or think. His Word tells us, "If you then, though you are evil, know how to give good gifts to your children, how much more will your Father in heaven give good gifts to those who ask him!" (Matthew 7:11). We can teach our children all the head knowledge in the world, but if we don't teach them the wisdom of taking up their cross and following Christ, what have we really accomplished? There is an eternal lesson plan that far exceeds any we will ever formulate here on this earth. That is the gift we should strive to give our children through our own example of sacrifice and obedience to God's plan.

FOR MORE INFORMATION ON THIS TOPIC

Warning: Nonsense Is Destroying America by Vincent Ryan Ruggiero (Thomas Nelson, 1994).

The Biblical View of Self-Esteem, Self-Love, Self-Image by Jay Adams (Harvest House, 1986).

Catholic Education: Homeward Bound by Kimberly Hahn and Mary Hasson (Ignatius, 1996).

The Christian Home School by Gregg Harris (Noble Publishing, 1995).

COUNT THE COST/REAP THE JOY

Our children are easily influenced. You should have the most influence in your child's life. Consider carefully the following questions:

1. What beliefs and truths do you want your children to hold onto?

_____

_____

_____

2. How well are you actively communicating those beliefs and truths now?

_____

_____

_____

3. Does your current situation cultivate or hinder the teaching of those beliefs and truths to your children?

_____

_____

_____

Why Homeschool? III

Belief: I can do a better job than the schools.

WHY, GOD, WHY? I questioned well into the night after another exasperating bedtime interrogation. I had been under the heat of a blinding light as our oldest son, only six years old, hammered question after question at me. "Are spiders really insects if they have eight legs?" "Why do so many books still say the brontosaurus was the biggest dinosaur when it was really the apatosaurus?" "Did you know Texas thought it was its own country before it became a state?" I begged off finally, waving my white flag of surrender (actually a T-shirt unimpressively left on the floor because he forgot to pick it up). I flopped into bed beside my husband and again questioned the plan of the Most High.

"Just because I have my master's degree in gifted education didn't mean He had to give us a gifted child," I complained.

"You mean two," Chip reminded, not looking up from his book.

Yes, two. Our youngest, four at the time, was already showing the symptoms. I call them symptoms because sometimes their giftedness reminds me more of something that needs to be treated. It is a mixed blessing. Both boys' thirst for knowledge seemed unquenchable, and it was all I could do to stay one step ahead of them. Certainly it was enjoyable to witness their passion for learning, but after all my years in special education teaching learning disabled and then gifted students, average became appealing. I admit,

I didn't even know what average looked, sounded, or acted like. I was hoping my own children would show me.

What I didn't know at the time was that God had prepared me to meet our children's educational needs from before they were born. I knew what a quality education entailed. I knew what it took to succeed in school. And I knew, for the most part, what to do if they ran into trouble along the way. Somehow, though, I believed the schools would be able to address the needs of each of my sons. I was wrong.

Do you have a child who is an early-bird learner? A child who learned to read early, talk early, or put 100-piece puzzles together at age two? Or instead, do you have a child who is a late bloomer? A child who at seven is still having difficulty remembering his sounds, avoids handwriting practice like it has the cooties, or has a great memory for math facts, yet can't add 1 + 2 by counting? Maybe you have a special needs child. One who has a diagnosed specific learning disability, AD/HD, or is emotionally fragile. Or you may have a child who has gaps in his/her learning. A child who by the time he reaches sixth grade still doesn't spell well (and you know it's because the school didn't emphasize spelling), who is below grade level in math/reading, or isn't challenged and is bored at school. All of these children need intervention. Schools are not set up to accommodate the needs of all children. But you, as their parent, having a strong conviction that they deserve the best education, can adapt teaching opportunities to their learning needs.

WHAT IS SUCCESS IN SCHOOL?

What is necessary in order to succeed in this world? That depends on what you believe constitutes success. As defined in the dictionary, *success* means "the favorable or prosperous termination of attempts or endeavors; the attainment of wealth, position, or the like." This definition makes me cringe! The definition of *succeed*, however, was more palatable: "to accomplish what is attempted or intended." What do you intend for your children? We have been called to "train up a child in the way he should go: and when he is old, he will not depart from it" (Proverbs 22:6, KJV). Your success as an educator means leading them where they should go. Your children's success comes when what they do points to God and not themselves. Their success may not even be seen or felt until adulthood. You are only accountable for yourself; your children will have to make their own choices. But no matter where they go to school, children can succeed. Your job is to set them up for success and not failure.

Certain principles encourage success in school:

• *Work "heartily"* (Colossians 3:23, KJV). All work, including schoolwork, should be done as unto the Lord. Reinforce that truth daily. Are your children in an environment where they are encouraged to give their accomplishments to the Lord?

• *Focus on things above* (Colossians 3:2). Where is your child's focus during the school day? Is he or she distracted by the trappings of his or her social life? Are your children focusing on whatever is true, good, and right (Philippians 4:8)? Does their environment blur or sharpen their focus on who and what is above?

God can be glorified, no matter the educational setting. But remember, your job, for which you will be accountable, is to prepare them to succeed God's way.

WHAT IS A QUALITY EDUCATION?

Quality is considered a level of excellence. It is understood that if you do a quality job, you go above and beyond the call of duty. We all desire a quality education for our children. School reform efforts focus on this very characteristic. But are the schools going above and beyond the call of duty for our children? Many believe they are. After all, they have taken on the role of parents in many places. They have become the family in many communities. Parents have relinquished their responsibilities in many ways, and the schools feel they have no choice but to pick up the reins if children are to move forward and learn. Most likely, *you* have not given up your responsibilities to your children, and yet your children will be under the same programs as children whose parents are absent in more ways than one.

You can provide a quality education for your own children. Parent educators go above and beyond the call of duty. It is a sacrifice, but a rewarding one, to teach one's own children in a quality manner. But the schools have also given up a great deal in their attempts to provide a quality education for all students, but this "sacrifice" is not a beneficial one. Actual teaching time has diminished as more and more programs have been squeezed into the school day. You will be able to give your children what they need in half the time of a traditional school day!

WE HAVE AN EARLY-BIRD LEARNER—NOW WHAT?

Some children learn sooner, faster, and more in-depth than others. Their ability to learn is noticed early in life. Many parents have children who speak in full sentences by fifteen months or teach themselves to read at four years old. Verbal ability is not the only indicator of an early-bird learner. Early evidence of artistic talent, being able to put 100-piece puzzles together at age two, and the ability to play a musical instrument with proficiency in the preschool years are all characteristics of a gifted learner. Their creative thinking is unmatched, or their logical thinking is unchallenged. Either way, as a parent you are in for an incredible ride!

"From everyone who has been given much, much will be demanded" (Luke 12:48, NIV) rings true in this circumstance. God has given all of us gifts and talents to use to bring Him glory. Parents must be keenly aware of such children's needs so they can help those children understand how to use their gifts to please God and serve His kingdom. For some of these early-birds school is torturous. It is an endless waiting game—waiting to be challenged, waiting to use their gifts. Many, including some teachers, mistakenly believe that gifted students will succeed whether or not they are challenged. But instead of success or excellence, the result is complacency. Making a habit of sitting on your laurels destroys the love of learning and is not pleasing to God. Children are not mature enough to overcome an environment that discourages innovative action or creative thinking. So it is up to us as their parents to place them where they can become proficient users of their gifts and talents. That place may be home. Again the idea is to set them up to succeed, not to fail.

WE HAVE A LATE BLOOMER LEARNER—NOW WHAT?

When Melissa was five years old, she still did not know her colors. This worried her mother, Jayne, because she knew the kindergarten requirements included color recognition. Was Melissa delayed in her development, or did colors simply not matter to her at that time? As your child's best teacher (which you already are), you know that answer. Sometimes as parents we lean too heavily on the words of the appointed experts. We dismiss our own instincts in favor of their advice. Parents know their children best. Put your trust in that fact. Comparing our children to the children of our friends, family, or peers is always a mistake. There were plenty of late bloomers throughout history who triumphed in the end and made incredible contributions to our world. Albert Einstein, Thomas Edison, and Leonardo da Vinci were all late bloomers. Traditional schools couldn't reach them. Each began to flourish when they were paired with mentors instead. In their own time they blossomed into extraordinary individuals.

Schools in our day and age work on a timetable. If a child doesn't progress along the prescribed time line, he is labeled as a slow learner, and some sort of intervention is usually recommended. When I taught learning disabled students, I was astonished to discover that many of my students had summer birthdays. In many states September 1 is the cutoff date for school entrance age. Kindergartners must be five years old on or before September 1. Summer babies, barely five, inevitably have a more difficult time adjusting to school. Some of these adjustments take years to accomplish. Some never catch up and then become labeled, but not before years of failure and discouragement.

Many choose to homeschool for this very reason. They have a summer baby or a child who is not quite ready, and they keep him or her home for the primary years of elementary school (kindergarten, 1, and 2) to better prepare them for school. Thus they are setting them up to succeed! Why would a parent want to do anything else?

WE HAVE A SPECIAL-NEEDS LEARNER—NOW WHAT?

"He's three and he's still not talking," Diana told her cousin, a teacher. After talking to her cousin, Diana decided to have her son tested for a speech and/or language problem. She wasn't sure anything was wrong, but she wanted to know if there was, so she could help him. "If he qualifies, he can attend the special preschool the public schools offer," Diana excitedly explained to her husband.

"I'm not sure I want him in formal school just yet," Dave said.

Diana's countenance fell because she didn't feel qualified to help her son should he need the extra help. Shouldn't she leave it up to the experts?

I was one of those experts, and yet I knew that what happened at home ultimately determined the success or failure of my program. My sister-in-law, a school speech therapist, says her heart breaks when she comes into contact with parents who do nothing to help their children improve. She knows, as I do, that what she does with them in the classroom is only a Band-aid; the real healing comes from a strong home with intense parental involvement.

You can work in partnership with the schools if you have a child with a diagnosed learning problem. If the program does indeed target your child's individual needs and desires a strong teacher/parent relationship, your child may do very well. However, the downside to this partnership is the fact that your child has now been labeled as an exceptional student for both legal and budgetary reasons. If you turn down the recommended program, you may be pressured to comply. In their defense, the schools really believe that your child's future is at stake. They do care, though their advice might not be best for your child.

One option that offers you more control is to have your child tested privately instead of through the school system. This way you control when and if the results are released and to whom. You may decide that your child is better off at home with you. Parents who choose to homeschool their special-needs child don't have to do it alone. NATHHAN (NATional cHallenged Homeschoolers Associated Network) is a Christian nonprofit network of families that encourage each other in the area of teaching special-needs children. They provide publications, directories, a lending library, and a parent learning center. Their newsletter (*NATHHAN News*) includes letters and articles from homeschooling families. Families thus find new teaching methods, products, and organizations. Professionals, excited about homeschooling, share tips. Families adopting special-needs children share inspiring stories.

As your child's parent, not only are you their best teacher, you are the expert they need most. There is plenty of support out there if you are motivated to homeschool your special-needs child.

THERE ARE GAPS IN OUR CHILD'S LEARNING—NOW WHAT?

"When do they start teaching spelling?" a parent asked me during our conference. Her daughter, a third grader in my part-time gifted class, was a terrible speller. I hesitated to answer her because I knew it would open a can of worms I wasn't convinced I could shut.

"What do you mean?" I asked instead.

"Jessica has never had a spelling test, nor has she ever brought home a spelling book. I remember taking spelling tests beginning in first grade. She's never going to improve this way." This parent was distraught. Her daughter was a victim of prolonged inventive spelling. Inventive spelling is a strategy introduced a number of years ago that educators hoped would encourage children to write without the fear of spelling something wrong. It was believed that children's creativity was stunted by the constraints of spelling. Unfortunately, we now have a whole generation of poor spellers.

Spelling isn't the only learning gap that can exist. Whether or not it is directly connected to a new teaching approach, over-crowded classrooms, or inept teaching, students fall through various cracks and are rarely rescued. Many parents try to fill the gaps by hiring private tutors or enrolling their child after school in a learning academy such as Sylvan Learning Centers. But for many this is cost-prohibitive. When I tutored students for these reasons, my goal was to work myself out of a job. I wanted them not to need me anymore. They needed to be able to transfer what I was teaching them into the classroom in order to be successful.

If your chosen strategy to fill in the gaps can't make the above claim, you are wasting your money and your child's time. As their parent who loves them more than any teacher or tutor ever could, you have the power to make a lasting impact on your child's learning experience. At home there are no time limits. If your child is having trouble learning his multiplication facts, you can keep going over them until he does. He doesn't have to move on until he's ready. So what if it takes him longer. The goal is to close those gaps!

How Can I Meet My Child's Individual Needs?

One of the most inspiring and motivating facts about homeschooling is the parent's opportunity to meet an individual child's learning needs. There are so many resources available now. There are a myriad of books giving how-to information, and there are hundreds of curriculum vendors from which to choose. No matter what you choose to teach, there are a few things to keep in mind. Know your child inside and out, and you will know how to teach him or her.

Learning Styles

How we learn is just as important to the learning process as *what* we learn. Whether your child is an auditory, visual, or kinesthetic learner or some combination will be a factor in how well he learns.

The key is to know how your child learns best, so that you can match your teaching style to his learning style. A more comfortable approach might be to teach your child in a variety of styles. That way he can learn the way he learns best but at the same time experience a subject in a way that may not be his preferred style. For example, teaching children about fractions can be done by explaining it aloud (auditory), drawing parts of the whole (visual), and cutting either a pizza or a pan of brownies (depending on your preference) into equal parts (kinesthetic). Choosing to do all three approaches will result in a real understanding of the concept.

Cynthia Tobias, author of *The Way They Learn*, offers helpful insight into learning styles. She provides an inventory for you and your children to help you discover your preferred learning styles.

Multiple Intelligence Theory

Howard Gardner has written extensively on the subject of Multiple Intelligence Theory. He proposes that there is more than one way to be smart. Which, if you think about it, is consistent with God's design. God has created a world full of diversity and variety. No two creations are the same. Therefore, there is no one way to define any one of them. Intelligence has long been associated with IQ tests. Gardner insists that we can be and are smart in at least seven ways: linguistic (word smart), logical (logic/number smart), spatial (picture smart), bodily-kinesthetic (body smart), musical (music smart), interpersonal (people smart), and intrapersonal (self smart).

Thomas Armstrong, another Multiple Intelligences author, has written material that focuses on the educational applications of this theory. In his book *Multiple Intelligences in the Classroom* (ASCD [Association for Supervision and Curriculum Development], 1994), he gives practical ways to view the educational process seven different ways. He also offers an inventory for adults and children to determine their prominent intelligences.

If your child is strong in logical smarts, then computer-assisted learning may be a good approach to his or her studies. If he is more linguistic, he may learn better either through the written or spoken word. Armstrong's book is full of ways to teach using the Multiple Intelligences. This is one more way to fully know your child and what he or she really needs in order to succeed.

Tailor-made Learning Experiences

With all this information about how your child learns, it is time to investigate his or her interests. Dorothy chose to bring her daughter Megan home to school when she was entering seventh grade. Megan's intense interest in horses and veterinary medicine became the focal point of their time. After spending time on basic skills, Megan goes to a stable each day to work alongside the trainer. In a year she has done the work of an apprentice, and her love for horses has increased even more. Watching her daughter apply her studies to what she loves most motivates Dorothy as her teacher to provide even more opportunities for Megan. During the years when many adolescents begin to waiver in their motivation to learn, Megan's has skyrocketed.

Find out what really interests your son or daughter. Then tie his or her learning experiences into that interest. That may change year to year, or it may be a lasting interest that goes on well into one's teen years and ultimately becomes his or her career choice in life. Such concentrated time like this can only be offered in a home-school setting.

IS HOMESCHOOLING THE ANSWER?

Your child was born with a unique set of learning needs. God did not make a mistake or forget to give your child necessary skills. His design is perfect. And He gave your child the perfect parents to teach him or her. He has already prepared you to meet your child's needs. You can provide that youngster with a quality education, one that will set him or her up for success. His or her success will then point to the Creator, not to you.

If you need help, trust God to provide it. He will bring people and resources into your life that will foster success. Your success as a teacher is linked to whether or not what you do pleases God. Make the choices that will bring success for you and your child, the kind of success that God favors and provides.

 DIANE

My friends had talked to me for years about homeschooling, but I had always quietly rejected the idea, thinking it was great for them, but certainly not for me. I loved my two daughters but felt the break we got from each other during school was good for all of us. It was my husband who first got interested in the homeschooling idea, which surprised me because my daughters were both enjoying the Christian school they attended. He asked me to just think about it. I wasn't exactly thrilled about it, but after some time I started praying and asked God to show me what He wanted me to do. I was almost afraid to tell my close friend who homeschooled, afraid that just the thought of me thinking about homeschooling would have her planning our next year together. Homeschool families are usually very vocal about their choice, and even that kind of scared me.

Well, halfway through my oldest daughter's second-grade year, a troubling situation began to emerge. Kelly had always had difficulty reading, not because she didn't try or due to a lack of effort on our part. She had a hereditary eye problem for which she had gone through extensive therapy. She began to hate to read aloud in class. She was not volunteering to give answers on anything. Her teacher told me she would just look down and put her hand over her mouth, so you could barely hear her. Kelly was smart, she had made Honor Roll several times, she was outgoing and social, but now . . . I felt God was showing me something. I began to think maybe I could help Kelly get her confidence back, help her with her reading one-on-one, maybe take some of the pressure off. I began to think maybe homeschooling was what Kelly needed.

My youngest daughter, Mikaela, would have to be homeschooled as well because I felt it would be too difficult running back and forth to school. Since they would only be a grade apart, I felt I could combine some subjects, and that might make it easier.

I have just completed my first year, and I am glad to report that

Kelly's reading has improved. But the "subject" that God has put on my heart for all of us is building our character and getting along with each other. Being at home has had its moments of great triumphs and agonizing adjustments.

The reason I continue to homeschool has changed from my original concern over Kelly and her confidence to read to building a strong family based on Christian character that I hope will go on beyond the schooling years. God has provided so many wonderful, teachable moments when we just stopped school and talked about what was going on. There were times school ended early because my character and attitude needed adjustment. I kid my friends and say I thought I was going to homeschool my kids, but God put me in my own homeschooling character study with Him! I learned a lot this year. I liked it more than I thought possible, and I am really excited about next year. But I still just plan one year at a time because that fits my personality, and thinking too far ahead always scares me.

For More Information on This Topic

NATHHAN (NATional cHallenged Homeschoolers Associated Network), 5383 Alpine Road SE, Olalla, WA 98359, (253) 857-4257

Multiple Intelligences in the Classroom by Thomas Armstrong (ASCD, 1994).

The Way They Learn by Cynthia Tobias (Tyndale House, 1994).

Count the Cost/Reap the Joy

1. How do you define *success* for your child?

_____

_____

_____

_____

2. Evaluate your child's current educational setting. Is he or she set up to succeed? Why or why not?

_____

_____

_____

3. In order to provide your own child with a quality education, you must count the cost. What sacrifices do you see you will have to make in order to homeschool?

_____

_____

_____

4. List here your child(ren)'s particular learning needs.

_____

_____

_____

5. Now list the ways homeschooling can meet those needs compared to traditional schooling.

_____

_____

_____

6. What questions do you still have about meeting your child's academic needs?

_____

_____

_____

How Long Should You Homeschool?

HOMESCHOOLING FILLS A variety of needs. The beauty is that it is flexible and forgiving, meeting children where they are and taking them on their own personal journey. How long that journey will last is an individual choice. There are many different perspectives on this. There are also a variety of considerations to take into account as you formulate your own perspective. Some journeys are as short as weekend getaways, while others may become lifelong voyages.

THE ONE YEAR AT A TIME APPROACH

Many first-year homeschoolers take this approach. The prospect of homeschooling kindergarten through grade twelve can be intimidating. What can also be intimidating is the question that even strangers ask you once they realize you homeschool: "How long do you think you'll do it?" My pat answer is always, "We're taking it one year at a time. Ask me again in June!" That often gets a laugh, but somehow I usually feel like I've made some kind of escape. Leaving that door open at the end of every year helps me not to get overwhelmed. However, there are cautions you should consider before choosing this approach.

How would you feel if upon hiring, your employer said to you, "Let's take it one week at a time and see how it goes"? What level of commitment has that employer made to you? Would you feel secure in your position? Would you wonder if one mistake could end your future there? Would you feel as committed to this job as you would to someone who promised to employ you until retirement? Would you work harder knowing it was going to end soon or if you were there for the duration? As parent educators in charge of our children's education, we are both employer and employee. What level of commitment are we willing to make to our children?

Recently we did a character study of the explorers Lewis and Clark. The trait that most illustrates their character is *perseverance*. We learned that perseverance meant to keep going even when you want to quit. If the ideal is important enough, you must persevere and see it through to the end. God will grant you such endurance if you ask for it. Much of what He calls us to do in this world is not easy.

Some circumstances lend themselves better to the one year at a time approach. Financially or physically you may be unable to commit to more than that. Whatever the reason, it is encouraging to know that the benefits of homeschooling affect children no matter how long or short a time they were schooled at home. This situation is similar to choosing to breastfeed your newborn. Even if you only nurse him for a couple of weeks, he has received the best nutrients, and that will affect his development long-term. Even though God created women's bodies in such a way that they can feed their children in the most nutritious and efficient manner, many choose other methods. Does this make them bad mothers? Of course not.

THE "WE'RE IN IT FOR THE LONG HAUL" APPROACH

The other end of the spectrum is to commit to homeschooling for the duration of children's school years. Many parents know, even before their first child is born, that they will homeschool their sons and daughters. Others pull their children out of traditional school during the elementary years with this same conviction. There's no looking back, no doubts, just full speed ahead. When asked the inevitable question about how long they intend to do this, they emphatically say, "All the way!" God has given them that assurance.

And on the days when they are frustrated and wonder what made them think this was a good idea in the first place, that assurance keeps them going.

A major concern to be considered with this approach is the danger of self-righteousness. This can manifest itself in a variety of ways. First, it makes it difficult to ask for help or consider other schooling options if you really need them. As an illustration, consider a woman (and her husband) who decided that natural childbirth was the only way to go and that if she did it right, she wouldn't need medical intervention. Then after twenty-four hours of no sleep, labor that was not progressing, and a husband who had fallen asleep in the bed next to her, she starts to wonder if an epidural might be a good thing. But she's afraid to ask and look like a failure at this childbirth thing. Just because you've chosen to homeschool for the duration doesn't mean that you can or should. You may need intervention; you may need a break.

Another way self-righteousness can get you into trouble involves how it affects others around you. Others just considering homeschooling may easily become intimidated by your resolve on how long one should homeschool. It may even be enough to frighten them away completely. If they feel you've communicated that it is an all or nothing decision, you have put a stumbling block in their way. As Christians we must be careful not to cause others to stumble. "Therefore let us stop passing judgment on one another. Instead, make up your mind not to put any stumbling block or obstacle in your brother's way" (Romans 14:13, NIV).

THE FILL IN THE GAPS APPROACH

This approach is the result of a family's initial reason to homeschool. Because there are gaps in their child's learning, they choose to homeschool in order to fill in those gaps. It may be that the child has a learning disability, is ADHD, or has missed many days of school due to illness or some handicapping condition. Either way, parents choose to homeschool to get their child up to speed and intend to place him back in a traditional setting as soon as possible. I have received much mail and E-mail from teens who for whatever reason have fallen behind and desire to homeschool in order to catch up without penalty. Some of this mail has come from teen mothers who want to stay with their babies but also desire to finish school.

Even though the intention here is to homeschool only long enough to catch up, many parents and children decide later that they can and should continue homeschooling. No approach is set in stone. Remember, the flexibility of homeschooling may be its greatest appeal. Stay aware of your child's needs. They may change, and then so may your choices.

WHEN THINGS CHANGE

No matter which approach you personally subscribe to concerning how long you intend to homeschool, realize that changes will challenge your resolve. Some result in a change for the better. Some are part of the spiritual battles you engage in daily and threaten to shut down your homeschool. God has promised the power of His Spirit to comfort you, help you to persevere, and enable you to discern truth when you hear it. Consider the following challenges. You may be experiencing some of them right now.

Economic Challenges

Cassie homeschools her four children, ages five to twelve. What started out as a one-year, fill-in-the-gaps solution has turned into a permanent commitment, something Cassie never would have predicted. But now that commitment is threatened. Her husband lost his job, and the church is buying their groceries. Cassie feels guilty, thinking that if she weren't homeschooling, she would have time to get a job of her own and put them on solid financial ground again. Her heart is broken. She doesn't want to leave her children. She doesn't want to work full-time. But if she can make ends meet by working, shouldn't she?

Cassie's situation is common. Many women who, after much soul searching, choose to homeschool suddenly find themselves in dire straits financially. Is this a sign that their choice was the wrong choice, or is it an attack from the adversary because she is doing exactly what God wants her to? If it is an attack, God has promised a way of escape. "There hath no temptation taken you but such as is common to man: but God is faithful, who will not suffer you to be tempted above that ye are able; but will with the temptation also make a way to escape, that ye may be able to bear it" (1 Corinthians 10:13, KJV). Wait on the Lord, and watch for His escape. This escape will allow you to continue in your obedience to God and at the same time attend to the immediate needs of your family. Cassie went into prayer and asked her ladies' discipleship group to pray that God would make it clear to her what He wanted her to do. Within twenty-four hours God provided both a new job (at less pay) for her husband and a baby-sitting job for Cassie in her home after her school hours with her own children. All this brought glory to God!

Concerns and considerations. There are some things you must keep in mind when faced with financial challenges. First, don't jump ahead of God. We tend to believe that we can solve the problem in our own strength. Be careful. Not only are you vulnerable to the sin of pride, but you could actually make things worse. God will humble you if you believe you can do this without Him. Another concern is: How are you to know if this is God's way of telling you He wants you to choose a different life and put your children back in school? You can know God's will by a three-pronged test: the surrounding circumstances, wise counsel, and His Word. If the change in direction is God's will, all three parts will fall into place to guide you. But if, for example, the circumstances seem to scream one thing, but wise counsel and God's Word say another, beware!

Emotional Challenges

Jan homeschools her two boys, ages eight and thirteen. She has always struggled with her oldest, Cary. By age five the school labeled him as ADHD. He was always in trouble and had no self-control. He is a very bright boy, yet has no common sense or organizational skills. Finally, when he was nine, she brought him home. She left her youngest in school for the time being. Every year she struggles with whether or not to put Cary back in school. His needs are so overwhelming and emotionally draining. She has no training and feels he is falling further and further behind. Her goals are to help him catch up academically and at the same time give him the structure and safe learning environment he needs. She feels these goals have yet to be met.

Jan chose to put Cary back into public middle school in eighth grade. She was so tired and defeated. But it didn't take long for her to realize this was a great mistake. The school put him into a special program with emotionally disturbed teens. Cary became more and more out of control and unable to focus. Any progress they had made at home together unraveled. At the same time the elementary school targeted Frank, her youngest, for testing for learning disabilities. Jan cried and cried. Her children were drowning! Should she bring them both back home? Could she handle homeschooling two boys with emotional and learning needs? Could she live with herself if she didn't?

Concerns and considerations. God will never give you more than you can handle. His power is at your disposal. The emotional challenges may be both your own and your child's. Beware of making a decision based upon feelings alone. Feelings are not reliable and should not be the overriding factor in decision-making. It is more important to know what God has to say about the situation. As parents we are called to provide a loving and safe learning environment for our children. "Fathers, do not exasperate your children; instead, bring them up in the training and instruction of the Lord" (Ephesians 6:4, NIV). If the environment in which they are learning is causing extreme anxiety or is provoking our children to wrath, it is our responsibility as parents to pull them out of such a situation. Jan is frustrated and exhausted from dealing with her children's emotional needs, but that does not mean she should put them back into public school. Even if they only do a little better while at home with her, that's better than becoming worse at school. Jan must go to the Lord to get her own emotional needs fulfilled. God will take care of the rest.

Academic Challenges

Cheryl's highly gifted daughter is already three grades ahead in her curricula. Cheryl believes it's only a matter of time before she will be unable to provide for Susan's academic needs. Susan knows exactly what she wants. She wants to become a doctor. All Cheryl can think of are the science and math courses she has absolutely no confidence to teach! Next year Susan will be in ninth grade. Maybe Susan should go to a traditional high school, one with an advanced track so she can get what she needs.

Maybe she should, maybe she shouldn't. Reaching the high school years doesn't automatically mean homeschooling is over. Parents of high schoolers feel intimidated whether or not their children are advanced learners. A parent who barely finished high school herself may feel intimidated by basic high school course work. Does that mean her child should go into a traditional school setting? What about the other end of the spectrum—a child who is severely learning disabled and unable to attain a regular high school diploma? Should he be placed in school so he can receive special course work or vocational studies? Granted, these are individual situations requiring individual decisions. I will not tell you what you can and can't handle.

Concerns and considerations. Consider first whether or not your child's academic needs can only be successfully met in the classroom. Are there no other options for him to pursue while at home? Are there no electronic classrooms (distance learning), co-ops, community college classes, or correspondence schools in which he can enroll? Have you investigated every possible option? You must do that first. Don't let your insecurities make this decision for you. The second consideration is whether or not your child is prepared emotionally and spiritually to excel in a traditional school setting. If not, being there will only frustrate him; and remember, God does not want you to frustrate your child.

Academic challenges are probably the easiest to address in the homeschool community. It is a matter of reaching out, admitting your needs as a teacher, and investigating possibilities. It may mean you take a community college class on the subject yourself before you teach it. What you will find, however, is that as you teach your child something you've never taken yourself, you learn right along with him. Surround yourself with other parents of high schoolers, and see what options are available.

CAROLYN

For me, it was an easy decision, almost too easy. I could go back to work as a teacher, teaching other people's children, or I could stay at home and invest my time, energy, and talent teaching my own children. I could have a boss or be my own boss. I could work at a school from 8-4, or teach my children at home in less than three hours a day. How could I lose? I couldn't lose financially, which is really the least important anyway. I couldn't lose morally or socially. Do I want my children's primary influence to be me or other children? And most importantly, I couldn't lose spiritually. How awesome a responsibility to be home with them day after day with a multitude of opportunities to teach them about Christ. (I feel the Lord convicting me here, of course, of the opportunities that were lost.) It's hard to lose when you home-school your children.

How has God confirmed this decision for me? Through my husband. God knew it was my heart's desire (of course, He put it there!). But I also knew I had to submit to the final decision of my husband, and he was not so easily convinced. He went to public school, and he turned out fine! I believe God answered my prayer. Rick saw how well the children responded to me academically but genuinely, in our overall relationship. He slowly began to see the fruits of having our children at home. And finally he went to a homeschool convention and heard a lecture on socialization. After the convention I was amazed as I watched him tell others why we are homeschooling our Kyle and Kaley. He was proud of it! And I was proud of him. Thank You, Lord!

There have been other confirmations as well, outward and inward. Just this year both of the kids told me how glad they were to be homeschooled. Our family is much closer, and the children get to see more of Daddy. Homeschooling may not last forever with us, but it is our choice for now. I have great peace in our decision, and I want to enjoy it thoroughly because it will be over before I know it.

How long will you homeschool? That question can have different answers, depending upon where God is leading you at the time. Circumstances may change. God may lead you on a different path, still within His will for you and your family. And His path for you may very well be different from someone else's path. If you believe you can only take this decision one year at a time, fine. If you believe wholeheartedly that your children will remain with you for their entire schooling experience, wonderful. Even if you know this is only a temporary solution to filling in your child's learning gaps, understand that it is the fact that you are willing to take responsibility for his learning that counts. How you perceive the situation may change. Your child's needs may change. But you need to stick close to God's Word regardless. Relying on your own sense of the right thing to do may lead you down a dark path. "Trust in the LORD with all thine heart; and lean not unto thine own understanding. In all thy ways acknowledge him, and he shall direct thy paths" (Proverbs 3:5-6, KJV). Since God's Word is truth, you can have complete assurance that He will indeed direct your path and that His paths are best!

FOR MORE INFORMATION ON THIS TOPIC

The Homeschooling Handbook by Mary Griffith (Prima Publishing, 1999).
Homeschooling the Middle Years by Shari Henry (Prima Publishing, 1999).

COUNT THE COST/REAP THE JOY

How long should we homeschool? The answer is different for each family and maybe even for each child in a family. As long as you are leaning on the Lord and not on your own understanding, you will make the right choice.

Let's take a moment to face each choice head-on.

1. List any concerns or obstacles you see to homeschooling one year at a time.

_____

_____

_____

2. List any concerns or obstacles you see to homeschooling long-term.

_____

_____

_____

3. List any concerns or obstacles you see to homeschooling just long enough to fill in some gaps.

_____

_____

_____

4. Now, which obstacles are too big for God?

_____

_____

_____

What to Say to Friends, Family, and Other Homeschoolers

I REMEMBER WHEN some of my friends decided to home-school. I bombarded them with many questions. To me they were burning questions asked out of curiosity, concern, and admittedly out of criticism. You will never be without probing questions if you choose to homeschool. It goes with the territory. We've already addressed the question of how long you intend to homeschool, but there are other questions that will come your way (if they haven't already). There are a variety of sources for you to consider when answering these questions, but I will give you in-a-nutshell answers that will calm your nerves and the worries of your concerned inquirers, some of whom are your friends, family, and even other homeschoolers.

THE SOCIALIZATION QUESTION

Prepare ahead of time for this one. This is probably the most commonly asked question about and to homeschoolers. "What about your kids' socialization?" My peers asked me that same question when I told them I had decided to stay home when our baby was born. The fact is, unless you intend to live in a cave, cut off from humanity, your child *will* be socialized. The key here is knowing what socialization even means.

According to the dictionary, *socialization* means "made fit for companionship with others." The goals of schooling are not goals of socialization. Socialization tends to occur outside the restraints of the classroom. You learn to get along with others when you engage in activities with others. The complete opposite is to be antisocial. Again, according to the dictionary, that means (1) adverse to companionship or to the society of others, and (2) opposed to the general good or basic principles of society. There is a long list of individuals who, despite being part of a large family and attending a public school, have still ended up antisocial. School is not the determining factor in whether or not an individual becomes socialized.

What They're Really Asking

Who asks this question? Everyone. What is the concern hiding behind this question? People are worried that your child will not be able to interact appropriately in a group, not be able to handle the stresses of living in this world, and/or will become antisocial. The fear is that your child will be too different to fit in. Isn't that interesting coming from a society that currently embraces a multicultural, multi-lifestyle, and multi-moral world? Which parts of this world do you want your child to fit into? Remember, we are called to live *in* this world, but not to be *of* it. We shouldn't really fit so well. We don't belong here. It is not our home.

What's Your Answer?

Over the years I've experimented with a variety of answers to the socialization question. It used to immediately put me on the defensive. Now it merely gives me the opportunity to ask the questions, so that maybe my listener will stop and think, even if for just a moment. I ask questions like: "What is your real concern about this?" "Wouldn't you like the chance to really teach your child how to socialize?" "What kind of person do you envision as a truly socialized person?" These probing questions will take the focus off your decision to homeschool and put it on the larger issue of children in today's society.

If you prefer to give an answer instead of asking a question, here are some examples.

- "Our children get along better now with each other and with outside friends than they ever did when they were in school."
- "I prefer to control with whom and in what situations our children are socialized."
- "It's nice to give our children the time they need to feel comfortable in new situations."
- "Our kids are more involved in outside activities now than ever before. They couldn't get more social!"

Expert Advice

Studies have compared the social behavior of homeschoolers versus their traditionally schooled peers. Although the results of most studies must be cited with caution, since statistics can be used to support just about anything you want them to support, the home-school environment seems to promote social harmony and positive relationships. Here are some of the previously cited social characteristics of homeschoolers:

- They get along well within different age groups, from babies to older adults.
- They rank high on self-concept scales.
- They adapt to new situations with relative ease.
- They are more involved in their communities.

Each of these characteristics reflects positive socialization. One mother, cited in Mary Griffith's *The Homeschooling Handbook*, puts it this way: "If I took a seedling, put it in a greenhouse, and then slowly acclimated it to the outdoors, it would thrive well—better than one started outside in the 'real' world—and better than one that was sheltered so much that the outside world was shocking. I feel we've got a good balance of our outside activities and friends, and lots of time to be together and do things as our interests dictate."

The real test is when you look at older teens and young adults from homeschooling families. Take the time to meet some, and most likely you will find that they have a strong sense of who they are and what they believe in and a desire to be a positive force in their communities. Isn't that what we all want for our children?

THE COLLEGE QUESTION

"Can your child get into a good college if he or she is home-schooled?" and "Can he qualify for scholarships?" are the two most common questions with regard to college and homeschooling. These questions don't only originate from the outside—you might ask them yourself. For that matter, so might your child. Our eldest son is a very goal-oriented individual. When he was in fourth grade, he wondered whether or not he could still qualify for college scholarships as a homeschooler. I assured him that he would have ample opportunity to compete for scholarships. The fact that he even asked the question assured me that we were on the right path.

What They're Really Asking

This question is usually asked by concerned people who are close to you. Additionally, those with older children now considering homeschooling have this same concern, since they are much closer to that deadline. People wonder how a homeschooler can maintain adequate academic records to present to a college. Will they have high school transcripts? Are they permitted to take the SAT or ACT? Will they be at a disadvantage because they were home-schooled?

However, many parents of homeschoolers are not at all concerned with this question. Their child might not even go to college. There are other options worth exploring.

What's Your Answer?

Your answer here is determined by how much you know about the current state of college admissions. The majority of major colleges and universities accept homeschoolers. In fact, some prestigious universities (for example, the Ivy League universities) scout them out. On more than one occasion *The Wall Street Journal* has run articles to this effect. So, can homeschoolers get into college? Your answer is a resounding "Yes!" but there is a "however."

Should all students go to college? That question begs to be asked, but in this day and age college is touted as the only viable option for a secure future. Students who attend vocational training usually do so by default. They are not "smart" enough to go to college, so they go to technical school instead. But homeschoolers are not surrounded day in and day out by the condescension of their peers. Together parents and students explore options according to God-given talents and expertise. Many homeschoolers know early on what career they want to pursue as adults and don't feel obligated to follow societal trends. Homeschoolers are not status-seeking individuals. Many do choose to go to college because their chosen field requires it. But they see college and vocational training as equally valid choices. Neither is Plan B or a compromise.

So if your child desires to attend college, he will have no problem getting in. If he instead chooses to apprentice or go into vocational training, he will also succeed. Without outside pressures, children will gravitate toward their natural gifts. Isn't that a wonderful aspect of homeschooling?

Expert Advice

Many homeschool web sites provide a link to colleges that accept homeschoolers. If college is in your child's future, there are some steps you can take to ease the admissions process. Sometime during the high school years it is highly recommended that your child secure transcripts. That may mean registering with an umbrella school that can provide such transcripts. It could also mean enrolling part- or full-time in a traditional school for that same purpose. Your area support group is invaluable during this time. These years can be ones of uncertainty if you don't take the time to plan. Homeschoolers are eligible to take both the SAT and the ACT. Again, investigate this probability within your support group or umbrella school for specific regulations.

Maintaining a portfolio with your child, especially through

middle and high school, will also facilitate the admissions process. Many colleges and universities accept portfolio assessment in lieu of or in addition to SAT/ACT scores. The key is to find out ahead of time what colleges are looking for and assemble the portfolio accordingly. Again your area support group can advise you and put you in touch with families who have already gone through this process.

Whether for college, apprenticeship, or vocational school, pre-planning is imperative. Take the time now to familiarize yourself with the policies and procedures involved in admissions into such programs. Involve your child in this planning as much as possible. After all, it is his or her future.

THE "WHAT MAKES YOU THINK YOU ARE QUALIFIED TO TEACH?" QUESTION

Many parents considering homeschooling silently ask themselves this question. "After all, I didn't go to college." "After all, I didn't train to be a teacher." "After all, I flunked algebra!" The list of reasons why they are not qualified to homeschool is quite long. It's bad enough that we say these things to ourselves, but when someone else, even someone we trust, says it aloud to us, we want to collapse in a heap on the floor!

I asked myself this same question during the deciding phase, but it devastated me more when it came from my own father. Why? Because he has always been my champion. He is my biggest fan and loves to brag about me. But he wondered whether or not I could give his grandsons what they needed for school. And I am a former teacher! But those credentials weren't enough, he thought. What's really interesting is that in the grand scheme of homeschooling, they really do mean nothing.

What They're Really Asking

This question is primarily asked out of ignorance. But on a more personal level, it is asked out of concern. Your family and friends desire the best education for your children, just as you do. They're simply not sure the homeschool package offers the best education.

What's Your Answer?

There's a good chance you'll immediately go on the defensive when asked this question. It's bad enough that you already had to wrestle with yourself about your answer to it. Now it's time to answer your critics, and some of them are closer to you than anyone else in your life. Your own spouse may be asking this question. Don't shed tears just yet. Take a deep breath and pray for wisdom.

If you feel led to give a detailed account of why you are actually uniquely qualified to teach your children, go for it. However, try not to apologize for your lack of skills, degrees, or diplomas. Concentrate instead on what you do have to offer.

- You love your child more than anyone else possibly could. A teacher may have affection, but she can't love your child like you do.
- You know your child better than any teacher can.
- Teachers have too many children and not enough hours in the day to really get to know them. You are willing to take as much time as your child needs to learn.
- Many children fall through the cracks in a classroom. There just isn't time to wait for stragglers to catch up. The teacher must move on regardless.
- You are 100 percent committed to your child's education. Teachers are committed to their students, but she is not 100 percent committed to yours.
- You are willing to continue to learn yourself so you can better teach your child. Even though teachers are offered workshops to continue to learn how to teach better, many don't have either the time or the inclination to take them.

Expert Advice

Many parents embarking on the journey of teaching a high school student are most concerned with the answer to this question. The issue of whether or not you are qualified to teach advanced math and science courses, for example, is ever present. There are ways to increase both your knowledge and confidence in subjects in which you feel weakest. First, as many veteran teachers will tell you, you can learn right along with your students. No one is supremely qualified to teach every subject. If you are admittedly weak in an area, it is your job to either improve that area or give the responsibility of teaching it to someone else. That may mean part-time enrollment in school, perhaps taking a class at a community college. It could also be that your child is more capable than you give him credit for and is competent enough to teach himself.

Whoever asks this question of you, even if it is yourself, needs to remember that God has already equipped you to follow His will for you. If He wants you to homeschool your children, He is faithful to provide you with whatever is necessary to accomplish that. Trust in Him.

THE "WHICH IS THE BEST WAY TO HOMESCHOOL?" QUESTION

Again this is something you yourself have probably already asked. In fact, you've probably already asked as many people who will listen! It is probably the question of least consequence. Yet homeschoolers themselves argue over the answer whenever they gather. If you are a new homeschooler, you desire to do things just right. That may be admirable, but it isn't advisable or helpful.

What They're Really Asking

Homeschoolers tend to be people with strong views. Sometimes we end up hitting people over the head with our opinions. Is schooling at home best? Are unit studies the better way to go? Is unschooling the true way to homeschool? The classical approach? The Bible as sole textbook? Advocates for each approach bombard new homeschoolers with their philosophies and curricula. The effect is usually a dizzying view of what homeschooling is all about. New homeschoolers leave a homeschool conference more confused and less sure of themselves than ever.

Maybe this is because for years homeschoolers have had to continually defend their choices. It's a reflex. But it doesn't have to be that way.

What's Your Answer?

The question may come more in the form of "What curriculum do you or will you use?" Your answer may change from year to year and from child to child. One size does not fit all. If I've learned anything from both my years in the classroom and from our awesome God, it's that there is not only one way to do just about anything. The only thing that has a clear path is our way to Him.

Yes, go to the homeschool conferences. Drink it all in. Just don't get caught up in the all or nothing philosophies you hear preached from the microphone during workshops—my own included. You are on a fact-finding mission while you're there. I know that many want to actually complete all their school shopping while at the conferences with their vast exhibit halls, but rushing into a curriculum just because you are on a proverbial high after one speaker's workshop is not wise. It may also cost you more than you anticipated.

Expert Advice

Your answer to this question should be formed according to the needs of your child and family as a whole. Go to the conference armed with a list of goals for your children. Listen carefully to speakers with whom you are comfortable. Choose materials based upon whether or not they will meet the majority of your children's needs. (More on curriculum in Chapter 10.) Be forewarned that not every child in your family will need the same things. And what you bought last year may not work for your next child. So when you are asked about what is the best approach to homeschooling, you can say with confidence, "Whatever works!"

CONCLUSION

There is no way I can give you a list of every question and answer that will come your way as you bring your children home. But the questions will come. As unavoidable as that may seem, the answers are simpler than you think. As with any answer, there is a danger of letting loose with words you will later regret. Pray that the Holy Spirit will help you choose your words and then guide your tongue.

The question that you must answer first before all others does not come from your family, your friends, other homeschoolers, or even yourself. It comes from the Lord. His question? "Do you trust Me?"

🍎 JUNETTA

When Josiah was about three months old, Joseph and I heard a radio interview with Dr. Raymond and Dorothy Moore on *Focus on the Family*. The program was on homeschooling; it intrigued me. Several weeks later one of the Moores' books, entitled *Home Grown Kids*, was read aloud on a weekday radio program on Moody Bible Network stations. My parents gave us that book for Christmas. It was filled with helpful parenting tips, anecdotes, and encouragement toward *Home Style Teaching*, which was another of their books that we added to our library. Joseph and I are both first-generation Christians, raising our children from birth in a Christian home. It has been very important to us to raise them in such a way that they will continue to pursue godliness and follow in the way of the Lord.

Having been raised by educators, and having loved school and the learning process, I enjoyed reading to and teaching my son, seeing how he learned, studying him, and watching him grow. By the time he was two years old, he could quote thirty-six Bible verses and seemed to understand them as he applied them to everyday experiences. What a joy and a blessing to have been given stewardship of this gift from God.

The year before Josiah was to enter kindergarten, I went to a home-school support meeting. My interest was rekindled, and the stove was stoked. I began reading everything on which I could lay my hands concerning home education.

When anyone asked me why I wanted to homeschool my son, my response was quick and sure: "I know my child better than any teacher does, and I believe I can do a better job teaching him one-on-one than one teacher can with twenty or more students in her classroom." If I was confronted with the question, "How long will you teach your children at home?" I answered more deliberately but with a little less confidence, "We are not sure; we will take it one year at a time."

Before the end of the first year, I hit my first bump in the road when I realized the vast difference between homeschooling and schooling at home. My confidence in what I considered my own intellectual prowess, abilities, and enthusiasm began to wane, and after my desperate cry for help, the Lord began to show me that my confidence and hope needed to be placed in Him, not in myself. What a difficult and yet wonderful lesson that was, and continues to be even after twelve years of home educating.

During the first two years of homeschooling, God began to develop within Joseph and me a conviction that we, as parents, are responsible for training up our children. Daily family devotions, "reading through the Bible in a year" programs, as well as seminars attended and books read all helped to reinforce our responsibility and commitment to train our children in godly character and to raise them in the "nurture and admonition of the Lord." Convinced that we were able to accomplish this more efficaciously at home, we ultimately decided against sending them away to school for six to eight hours a day. A friend so aptly stated, "What you cannot pay another to do for money, a parent will do for love."

The challenges have been multitudinous over the years, and sometimes overwhelming, but the Lord has always delivered us, causing us to overcome and grow as a result. There have been times when I thought I could not continue, and there have been times when I thought I did not want to continue, but there has not been one time that God has not confirmed His will for me to continue. Whether in a Scripture passage, a passage read in a book, a radio program, or a pastoral teaching in what may seem to be an obscure Bible text, God comes through. I have received encouragement and counsel from friends when we have shared common struggles. Both friends and strangers, unaware, have encouraged me through their personal testimonies. Focusing on my purpose and goals in life has helped bring my focus back onto the philosophy of education

I developed during the time God was developing within me the conviction to home educate.

Not allowing discouragement and despair, and persevering during difficult times results from daily dying to self and taking up my cross and following Him. This is how I find confidence, peace, and rest in this awesome responsibility.

FOR MORE INFORMATION ON THIS TOPIC

The Successful Homeschool Family Handbook by Dr. Raymond and Dorothy Moore (Thomas Nelson, 1994).

The Homeschooling Book of Answers by Linda Dobson (Prima Publishing, 1998).

101 *Devotions for Homeschool Moms* by Jackie Wellwood (Crossway Books, 2000).

COUNT THE COST/REAP THE JOY

Education is a process of questioning and answering. As you consider and reconsider homeschooling, questions will come at you from without and from within. The best course of action is to ask yourself some questions first.

1. Who will or does take exception to your choice to homeschool your children?

_____

_____

_____

2. What are their greatest concerns?

_____

_____

_____

3. Why do they have these concerns?

_____

_____

_____

4. How can you ease these concerns?

_____

_____

_____

Try not to become defensive. Most often it will be just a matter of time before the strength of your testimony wins them over.

What If I Have Doubts?

MOST HOMESCHOOLING proponents don't like to mention the *d* word. But it is a reality and should be addressed. If you don't have doubts periodically, you're not serious about what you're doing. Homeschool families experience a myriad of doubts. Some are based in reality; some are not. Some deserve further investigation, some require continual prayer, and some should just be dismissed. Parenting is not an exact science, and neither is teaching. Doing either well is considered an art in some ways. You need to look at your inner doubts, face them, and then make some calculated decisions. Do even former teachers-turned-homeschoolers have doubts? Yes. No one is immune.

Although doubts may vary from family to family, there are a number of them that many homeschoolers share.

"I DON'T THINK I CAN MEET THE UNIQUE NEEDS OF MY CHILD AT THIS TIME AT HOME"

The beauty of homeschooling is its flexibility. You can tailor your teaching to each child. But if you have more than one child, you may feel the way most teachers do trying to accomplish the same thing—it is difficult to meet the needs of every student. You're afraid one won't get what he needs. You feel inadequate and definitely not up to the task. Let's consider some variations on this situation.

You may have homeschooled for years, but now your oldest is in the middle school years, and you question whether or not you can prepare him for high school or beyond. This doubt is worth further investigation. You may be more equipped than you are giving yourself credit for, or you may be right—your child needs more than you can provide. However, this doesn't mean you should send him back to school. It means you may have to do some homework of your own. Investigate the possibilities for this age group; hook up with other homeschoolers with children the same age. Listen, learn, and then choose the best course.

You have a special-needs child who requires extra attention, a totally different approach, or a different environment. You may believe that the "experts" in this area at the school are better qualified to meet the educational needs of your child. I know it is scary to face something outside of normal, but you'd be surprised how well most children with special needs do at home with their parents as opposed to a classroom with others with those same needs. No one will love your child as much as you do or will be able to give him the attention he both deserves and requires. Most likely your doubts stem from being alone in your questioning. Surround yourself with other homeschoolers with children like yours and be encouraged. It can be that simple.

What if your child is gifted and incredibly ahead of anything you give him? Wouldn't he be better off in a school or class with others like himself, so he could be challenged? If such a perfect place exists, that would be wonderful. However, the truth of the matter is that even in a gifted classroom, teachers are overworked, overwhelmed, and overrun with students. There is no time to meet individual needs on that front either. You have more time and have access to more resources for your gifted child than any teacher could have. Educate yourself about the nature and needs of gifted children, attend parent conferences, and join a gifted organization such as the NAGC (National Association for Gifted Children). You are definitely not alone.

What if one child is a homebody, but the other is incredibly social? Shouldn't the latter be in school so he can be around his peers more often? This doubt is imposed by society. You still wonder about the socialization issue, don't you? Ask yourself where most socialization occurs. It shouldn't be happening during class time, as any teacher will tell you. It happens in the lunchroom, on the playground, or at club meetings and other extracurricular events. Your social butterfly will have more than adequate stimulation when you go to church, youth group, scouts, book club meetings, baseball, soccer, 4-H, and lessons of all kinds. And you will be able to choose within which environment you want your child socialized, as every parent should.

It is true that homeschooling is not for everyone, nor is it for every child in every family. You must decide what is best for your own family. Just be sure you are making the choice and are not letting your doubts make it for you.

WHAT IF THEY DON'T TEST OUT WELL?

As a diagnostician who evaluates homeschoolers, I know that question causes anxiety and even nightmares for many parents. Facing the realization that you are 100 percent responsible for your children's education can be intimidating.

My child has never taken a standardized test before. What if he chokes? If your state requires that your child take a standardized test, or if you have decided that is the best evaluation alternative available to you, there are a variety of ways to accomplish this. First, your child can take it in a regular public school classroom where you are zoned. If your child attended that school previously, this may be an appropriate choice and put him at ease. Second, your child may take it with other homeschoolers at an umbrella school at a predetermined place and time. Lastly, he could take it individually either with a certified teacher or a psychologist who offers this kind of testing, and in some states with you. No matter which way you choose, it may be your responsibility to ensure that a test is ordered for your child ahead of time. This is usually done by the end of February. Choose a setting in which your child will be most comfortable.

My child has a learning disability, and a standardized test form would be too distracting to him. Test-taking skills are especially valuable to a student with a learning disability. If your child's particular weakness affects his test-taking ability, there are alternative ways to administer such a test. If enrolled in a public school learning disabilities program, he would be able to have test modifications. For example, if your child has a reading disability, all or portions of the test could be read to him by an objective party. Another avenue would be to have him tested by a certified teacher either in your home or in her home. This more relaxed setting may be all he needs. Time limits may also be extended for the learning disabled child. Check with the test administrators, and ask what modifications are available to your child.

You could also help prepare your child for the test environment and the form of the test by doing practice sessions using practice tests that can be purchased either from the publisher or provided by the school or agency administering the test to your child.

I don't want my child involved in standardized testing. Can we avoid it? The majority of states use standardized testing merely as one option for evaluation. There are some states that require it. Check your state's guidelines by visiting www.hslda.org. Some parents don't want their child's scores reported as part of the district's results. What you may not realize is that many districts do not include homeschool students' scores in their reporting. So you have nothing to worry about. However, if they do and you do not want them reported, you might prefer to choose someone else to administer the test.

If you don't want your child to take a standardized test at all, that is perfectly acceptable as long as it is permissible with the authority to which your homeschool answers. Ponder your reasons for not wanting this testing. If you are required, then it is important that you comply with your state, district, or umbrella school's regulations.

If my child does not perform at grade level, will the state make me put him back in a school? Homeschooling is quite mainstream at this point. Many, if not all, states will not pull a child from his or her home to go back to a traditional school. If your child does not perform at grade level for an extended period of time, the state or district may ask to see your curriculum. Some even offer assistance to help you bring your child up to grade level. However, the schools are having the same difficulty. That's why national standards now state that "all children will perform at or above grade level." You could turn the tables and ask what happens when regular schoolchildren don't perform at grade level. No one pulls them from school to be homeschooled! Your concern here is valid, but don't blow it out of proportion. Target your child's weak areas, and do whatever it takes to help him or her learn. You have all the time and love at your disposal. Your child will not be put in a lower group or in a remedial program. He'll have you. What more could he or anyone else ask?

What does "adequate progress" mean? Many state/district guidelines for homeschooling include the statement, "Evaluation should show adequate progress." What that means is, did the child progress from his last evaluation? Even when your child is below grade level, if he progresses in any one area at all, that is adequate progress for that child. Each child is different, and his progress is gauged individually.

Two issues regarding testing are important for you to consider. First, is it necessary in the first place? There are normally a variety of options when it comes to homeschool evaluations. Standardized testing may be one of those proposed options. It is your choice. You have to ask yourself why you want standardized testing for your child. For some it is a matter of comparing the two programs. Your child took a standardized test last year when he was in school, and you want to see how well your homeschool program did in comparison. But remember, your methodology is different from his school's; so the results may also differ. A child's adjustment to a new program or setting can easily bring lower test scores. But if your child has never been in a traditional school setting and you are choosing standardized testing, be clear as to why. You may think you should just in case you put in him school someday. But it isn't necessary.

Second, what will you do with those results? What if you don't like what you see? Are you required to file them with the district/state? You may want to consider that necessary evil first before even signing your child up to take such a test. If, on the other hand, you are looking to those results to help you make informed curriculum choices for your child, maybe it's worthwhile. It depends on the test. You want something that can tell you in its analysis what kind of errors your child made. Not all states report their results this way.

The bottom line is that standardized testing is not inherently good or bad. It is only one tool you have at your disposal to provide the best education for your child. Don't let it frighten or discourage you.

WHAT IF MY CHILD WANTS TO GO BACK TO SCHOOL?

Sarah's fifth-grade year was torturous for both mother and daughter. She constantly begged to go back to school. She had only attended kindergarten in a traditional setting; so Sarah's mom wasn't even sure her daughter remembered what school was like. Sarah said she was tired of being different and wanted to be with her friends. Most of her friends from church went to a private school, and Sarah felt left out. This was their fifth year homeschooling. Sarah's mom just wasn't sure it was time for her daughter to be away again. After one teary conversation with a good friend who homeschooled both her children completely until college, Sarah's mom was told that the fifth year was one of the hardest! Whether that was true or not didn't matter. But it was encouragement enough for them to keep homeschooling. She told her daughter that she felt convicted when she first chose to bring Sarah home to school and that she didn't feel that same conviction to put her back. "Until God tells me otherwise, we'll homeschool."

Is it okay for her to go back just because she wants to? All children go through periods of letting go, and for homeschoolers that may surface in the form of wanting to go to "regular" school. That may indicate they need more opportunities away from you in a safe setting. They need a chance to be responsible with what they've already learned from you. They need a chance to grow on their own. That doesn't necessarily mean school is the right place. In fact, it may be the worst possible place for them to explore their independence. It is still up to you to provide them with safe circumstances. Only you know where that place is.

We are miserable together right now. Wouldn't we all be happier if she went back? Pay now or pay later. Sending her back to school just so it will be more peaceful at home is a Band-aid solution. All it does is create distance; it does not promote harmony. Bite the bullet. Hang in there. Fight the good fight. Finish well. All these clichés actually have validity in this situation. If you are having trouble getting along because your child wants to go back to school, the problem is deeper than homeschooling. The problem lies in your relationship. Being home gives you the opportunity and time to work on that relationship. Spending less time together will not improve it.

What will her adjustment be like if she goes back to school? If you do decide to allow your child to go back to regular school, be prepared for an adjustment period. It will all depend upon how long she was homeschooled. She will realize quickly that her time is not her own. She will have to adhere to strict timelines and restrictions. She will have to meet expectations that are sometimes higher and many times lower than what she is used to. The social pressures may feel unmanageable at times. You need to be available to her more now than ever. She needs to know that home is a safe place, a haven.

WHAT IF I AM A SINGLE PARENT?

If you are choosing to homeschool and you are a single parent, first of all, you deserve applause! Single parenting is difficult at best, and homeschooling as a single parent requires more support. It will not be easy, but it will definitely be worth it.

I work during the day. How can I homeschool? If you are set on homeschooling and you work during the day, you may have to consider child-care of some sort until you get home. Homeschooling does not adhere to the clock or the days of the week. If you have a teenager at home, he or she may be able to work alone, utilizing either distance learning or a co-op of sorts until you return to work with him or her on the more difficult subjects.

Is it worth investigating an at-home business? If you are willing to lower your standard of living in order to stay at home, you may be able to work as a consultant of some kind or run a business out of your home. This will take some careful investigation and some lifestyle changes. Sacrifices will have to be made, but your child is worth it.

Is there a way someone else can teach my children instead? Some states allow for a certified teacher to teach a number of children in her own or someone else's home. Some allow any home educator to do so; however, that person would most likely have to establish him- or herself as a private school and adhere to specific guidelines. Again, this requires research and networking. Check with your local support group about hiring a teacher.

It is not impossible to homeschool if you are a single parent. In fact, there are even single dads who homeschool their children. Go to your state's homeschool convention and you'll meet some of the most amazing single parents. They'll inspire you and become lifelines!

What If I Want to Put My Children Back in School?

Sometimes you yourself will decide that you want your child to attend "regular" school. There is an assortment of reasons for this choice. However, be sure that it is in your child's best interest and not just your own. After all, God willing, you will be around long enough to do what you want to do after they're grown.

What if my child is still struggling, no matter what I do? Have you sought after and obtained help in their area of weakness? Trying to go it alone is foolish. However, even if you have tried everything at your disposal, what makes you think he will do any better in school in a classroom of thirty including some major discipline problems? His struggle may even go unnoticed. Are you willing to take that chance?

What if an opportunity I have waited for has finally come? The army's former slogan, "Be all that you can be," is very inspiring. What does that mean for you? You may think you have an opportunity of a life-time, one you can't possibly pass up. Remind yourself of why you chose to homeschool in the first place. Is the need that you identi-fied as the catalyst for this choice now met? Have you finished this work? For everything there is a season, as we read in Ecclesiastes. King Solomon knew that, and he also knew that everything we do, unless it is to please God, is vanity. If this new opportunity is truly from God, it will be confirmed by circumstances, wise counsel, and His Word. If not, it is vanity. Choose carefully.

Can one child go to school and one stay home with me? Homeschool situations vary as much as the children themselves. That's the beauty of it. Every child is different and has a different set of learn-ing needs. You may be called to homeschool only one of your chil-dren, and that's fine. You don't need permission from anyone to do that. You know what is best for each of your children.

WHAT IF OUR CURRICULUM CHOICE ISN'T WORKING?

So much of the homeschool curriculum is only available through vendor catalogs. And you can't thumb through textbooks found in catalogs. It's important that you not only have an opportunity to look through the curriculum yourself before you buy it, but also that you talk to others who have used it. Testimonials aren't fool-proof, but they can help in your decision-making. Most of us don't have money to waste; so the money you spend on curriculum must be a careful investment.

I'm not an education expert. Maybe it's my fault this curriculum isn't working. Yes and no. Yes, you may not be using the curriculum correctly. Maybe you require additional training. If you still like it, then seek out that training. Contact the vendor, and ask about workshops in your area. However, maybe it is just a matter of a poor match. Perhaps the curriculum didn't live up to your expectations because it didn't match them in the first place. Sell it at a used curriculum sale, cut your losses, and move on. This time make sure you are clear on what you expect, and make sure the curriculum matches your needs and expectations.

If this curriculum isn't working, how can I know the next thing I choose will work? None of us wants to throw money away. For some, our resources are quite limited. Don't buy something just because it's packaged well or because your best friend swears by it. And never buy anything sight unseen. Again, go to used curriculum sales and thoroughly check it out before you buy. You may also find that one curriculum works for your oldest but fails miserably with your youngest. You must tailor the curriculum to the needs of the child using it. First make sure you know your child's needs.

Is it okay to use no curriculum? Some homeschoolers call themselves unschoolers and do not utilize a formal curriculum. However, some unschoolers do utilize some boxed curricula and create the rest themselves. It honestly does not matter what you use as long as you know what your child needs and find the best way to meet those needs. We use an eclectic approach—a combination of textbooks, unit studies, and hands-on learning. I sometimes choose different things for different children. It depends on what they need. Allow yourself the freedom to choose. You're in charge!

Just as a little stress is good for your body, a few doubts can be good for your homeschool experience. They keep you on your toes. It shows you are asking yourself, "Why am I doing what I'm doing?" before someone else does. The danger is when you allow those doubts to plague your mind and make your decisions for you. You end up focusing on the doubts more and more and less and less on your children. Unresolved doubts will steal your joy.

VICKI

When I announced to my family and friends that I was going to pull our children from their public school in order to homeschool them, I was met with some surprising responses. Since most of my friends were already homeschooling, they considered me the last holdout. They were ecstatic! My parents, on the other hand, were not so happy. They didn't disapprove—they just didn't understand it. I am a former public school teacher, and my parents were always proud of my accomplishments as an educator. But for some reason they weren't sure I'd be able to give my children what they needed at home. Their concerns surprised me since they had been so fond of bragging about my teaching prowess for years. How could they be worried?

My friends' response also caused me to wonder. Yes, they were happy that we were homeschooling, but they kept telling me how easy it would be for me and how I wouldn't have the same problems as every other beginning homeschooler because I was a teacher. In fact, they were looking forward to my helping them to teach better. That I am happy to do, but to assume that I would have no problems only caused me to doubt myself.

Even my husband thought homeschooling would be a piece of cake for me. When I would voice my concerns, he'd tell me that I of all people had nothing to worry about. He didn't take any of my concerns seriously either.

Being a former teacher and now a homeschooler is not a piece of cake. I am probably more aware than most of how overwhelming this responsibility can be. Yes, I taught public school, but I have never taught second grade or fourth grade—and certainly not at the same time! I wasn't sure what curriculum was best. It was trial and error for me too. The problem is that when I do have doubts (and I have them frequently), I feel I have to keep them to myself because of everybody's high expectations for me. I feel as if I'm not allowed to doubt myself.

I loved teaching, and I loved school. It was hard for me to break that cycle by taking our children home. I still wonder if this will always be the best choice for them. We take it one year at a time. There are days when I look at our boys and am convinced they don't belong anywhere else, but there are also days when I wonder why I thought I could do this in the first place. But for now I'll keep those doubts to myself.

FOR MORE INFORMATION ON THIS TOPIC

The Homeschooling Book of Answers by Linda Dobson (Prima Publishing, 1998).

The Unschooling Handbook by Mary Griffith (Prima Publishing, 1998).

A Parent's Guide to Standardized Tests in School by Peter W. Cookson, Jr., and Joshua Halberstam (Learning Express, 1998).

N.A.G.C. (National Association for Gifted Children), 1707 L St., N.W., Suite 55, Washington, D.C. 20036; (202) 785-4268; www.nagc.org.

Home School Legal Defense Association (HSLDA), P.O. Box 3000, Purcellville, VA 20134; www.hslda.org.

COUNT THE COST/REAP THE JOY

> **D**angerous
> **O**bstacles
> **U**ndermine even the
> **B**est
> **T**eachers

No one is exempt from experiencing doubt. Your doubts may have brought you to this book in the first place. What you *do* when you are attacked by doubt is important. You are able to combat it. The problem is that many homeschool advocates refuse to acknowledge the *d* word, and so any homeschooler who is experiencing doubts is afraid to talk about them. Don't worry, the homeschool police will not come after you if you reveal your doubts!

1. What doubts about homeschooling are you having that are strong enough to influence your decision-making?

_____

_____

_____

_____

2. What is the worst thing that could happen if these doubts came to pass?

_____

_____

_____

3. Sometimes doubts are symptomatic of double-mindedness. If you are to benefit your children while homeschooling, you must commit yourself to them. In that sense there is no room for doubt. You need to talk to other homeschoolers whom you trust and respect and from whom you can gain wise counsel. Pray for confirmation of your choice. Ask God to make clear to you what He wants you to do.

PART II

THE BASICS

What Are the Rules for Homeschooling?

THE BOYS WERE EXUBERANT after a trip to the library. Their excitement was hard to muffle as I drove home. But the cruiser's lights and sirens broke through, and I realized to my horror that they were directed at our car! I pulled over, and in less than a moment I was completely overwhelmed, though I promised myself I wouldn't cry. You see, I am not a rule-breaker by nature. I wasn't upset that I was caught breaking a rule. I was upset because I did it at all, albeit unintentionally. I listened carefully as the officer described how fast I was traveling. I apologized, but not without offering an excuse. "You see, we're new to the mountains, and I haven't yet figured out how to navigate these hills per the posted speed limit." He didn't care. And he wasn't through. Not only had I been speeding, but when he checked my registration, he found that I hadn't had the emissions tested yet. Then when I went to retrieve my insurance card, it was missing. Another strike against me! There were explanations for everything. One that claimed foolishness, one that claimed ignorance, and one that could only claim carelessness.

Now would be a perfect moment for those tears, but all I could think about was that our sons were sitting in the backseat intently focused on our conversation. At that moment I realized how much they would learn from witnessing this very common yet unsettling situation. I humbled myself before the officer, willing to accept any consequences. The officer gave me a steep ticket and a warning. I thanked him and drove home at the posted speed limit, watching as every other car raced by me.

This experience reopened my eyes to the importance of submitting to our God-given authorities. As homeschoolers we are under certain authorities, whether we like it or not. Homeschooling laws vary from state to state. It is part of the responsibility of homeschoolers to investigate, familiarize themselves with, and adhere to that law without any excuses of foolishness, ignorance, or carelessness. There are general practices I can share with you in this book, but each state is different, and it is your responsibility to know the law in your state (as the officer so succinctly reminded me). Not only is it important for your own sake, but for the sake of homeschoolers everywhere, as well as for the sake of your children. They're watching and listening to every word. What will you teach them through all this?

General Policies and Procedures

Statutes addressing the issue of homeschooling cite the following eight expectations. A brief explanation of each follows.

• *Compulsory school age.* At what ages are children required to be in school? More specifically, how old should they be when they start and how old when they can stop? Be aware that many states are opting to change the compulsory school age in a responsive action of educational reform that affects both starting and/or stopping ages. The belief is that the more years children are in school, the better they will do.

• *Option to homeschool.* Homeschooling is legal in all fifty states, and this is specifically stated in state statutes.

• *Length of school year.* How long should your school year be as a homeschooler? Some states require a specific number of days. Some even dictate how many hours per day children should be schooled. What usually interests me is that some states require more of homeschoolers than they do of public schoolchildren.

• *Subjects required.* What should you teach? The state often requires more than the three R's for homeschoolers. Some are very specific and may include the Constitution, health, etc. Some states require very little, and it concerns me that they don't have high standards—not just for homeschoolers, but for anyone.

• *Teacher qualifications.* This clause varies tremendously from state to state. Must you hold a teaching certificate in order to homeschool? Some states say yes. Some states offer options for both certified and noncertified teachers. Others permit the hiring of a private tutor in lieu of the parent educator. Pay close attention to this clause. Know what it says.

• *Notice required.* The reason there isn't an accurate account of how many homeschoolers there really are is because we have not stood up to be counted. The law itself makes this more difficult. Many states require that homeschoolers register with their particular school district, so the state can keep track of their numbers. Other states offer an alternative. You may register either with your zoned district or an umbrella school (a private school willing to keep track of your child). But many homeschoolers choose neither option and go uncounted. I strongly recommend that you adhere to your state's law and register. All this means is that you file a letter of intent with whatever authority your state requires. This must usually be done within a specific time period before you begin homeschooling.

• *Record keeping required.* This clause also varies considerably from state to state. Some states expect you to keep strict attendance records and lesson plans. Others require no record keeping. Even if you are required to keep track of your attendance (the days and hours you "do" school), there are a variety of ways to accomplish this. It's fair to assume that various homeschool families do their record keeping differently. It is usually less cumbersome than the statute outlines. In this case the law is not dictatorial but guiding.

• *Testing required.* Again, this clause differs from state to state in its options and expectations. Some states do not require any testing. Others require exactly what the public schools do. Still others offer a variety of testing/evaluation options. For example, Florida state law outlines five different evaluation options for homeschoolers. That's wonderful, especially if you consider that public school students have only one option.

The law is very clear when it comes to homeschooling. Your area support group may even offer a workshop on explaining and adhering to the law. Your state probably has a homeschool lobbyist who works hard to keep the law friendly and to inform you when changes are proposed. However, what it comes down to is your willingness to obey the law. As a Christian, you are expected to submit to your governing authorities as long as they do not lead you into sin. That does not mean you will always agree with the current law. There are ways around the law, but that process is similar to the one my husband and I teach our own children. If we tell our children to do something, and yet for some reason they either can't obey or do not wish to, they have the option of appeal. However, in order for their appeal to even be heard, we must first see their intent to obey. We are much more willing to listen to their appeal, although with no guarantee that we will change our mind, when we see that they intend to obey us regardless.

DIFFERENT STROKES FOR DIFFERENT STATES

As previously stated, every state interprets the right to homeschool differently. They range from a complete hands-off approach to being more involved than we'd wish. The HSLDA (Home School Legal Defense Association) has categorized states according to their levels of regulation with regard to homeschooling. The law is in a constant state of flux, but the states fall roughly into the following categories:

• *Low.* In general, this category describes the state's involvement as low regulation, with no requirement for parents to initiate any contact with the state: Idaho, Illinois, Indiana, Michigan, Missouri, New Jersey, Oklahoma, Texas.

• *Moderate.* Moderate regulation usually means the state requires parents to send notification, test scores, and/or a professional evaluation of student progress: Alaska, Alabama, Arizona, California, Colorado, Connecticut, District of Columbia, Delaware, Florida, Georgia, Hawaii, Iowa, Kansas, Kentucky, Louisiana, Maryland, Mississippi, Montana, North Carolina, Nebraska, New Hampshire, New Mexico, Ohio, Oregon, South Carolina, South Dakota, Tennessee, Virginia, Wisconsin, Wyoming.

• *High.* These states require parents to send notification or achievement test scores and/or professional evaluation, plus other requirements (e.g., curriculum approval by the state, teacher qualifications of parents, or home visits by state officials): Arkansas, Massachusetts, Maine, Minnesota , North Dakota, Nevada, New York, Pennsylvania, Rhode Island, Utah, Vermont, Washington, West Virginia.

Suggestion: Check out your state's law regarding homeschooling at the HSLDA website: www.hslda.org. Please understand that nothing in this book is intended as legal advice.

WHY SOME OF US DON'T OBEY THE LAW

Whether we agree with the law or not should not determine whether or not we obey it. Yet some of us have inadvertently disobeyed the law or parts of it. Your response when this happens is important. What testimony do you want to leave with the governing authorities? What testimony do you want to leave with your children? I didn't set out to speed that day, and yet I did. Some people, however, speed with total disregard for the law.

Out of Foolishness

Who is a fool? According to the Bible, a fool is someone who does not believe the truth of the Gospel. "The fool says in his heart, 'There is no God'" (Psalm 53:1, NIV). Such persons choose to disregard God's authority in their lives and sometimes bring others along with them. We act out of foolishness when we do not believe the truth of the law of the land, which God has commanded us to obey (Romans 13:1). We walk around thinking that somehow it doesn't apply to us. And we lead others down this same path of foolishness. This is something I come into contact with both at homeschool conventions and while in homeschool chatrooms online. Many people, including homeschool parents, somehow think they are not obligated to obey the law. This is a poor testimony, to say the least. Jesus commanded that we give Caesar Caesar's due. Do you?

Out of Ignorance

Can you claim ignorance of the law? Believe it or not, no. It is every person's responsibility to know the laws under which they live. So if you move to a different state, most likely the laws will be different. It is part of your responsibility as a homeschool parent to educate yourself about your state's laws. The state government may choose to show mercy because of your ignorance, but it is not required to. It is better to be informed than to have to claim ignorance if you are rebuked.

Out of Carelessness

When our children make careless errors in their math, are they still wrong? Certainly. However, if they catch their mistake before it is noticed and correct it, they are prudent. We too are accountable for our carelessness. We know better. "But I tell you that men will have to give account on the day of judgment for every careless word they have spoken" (Matthew 12:36, NIV). God will expect an account. So will the state.

Out of Defiance

Defiance means wanting your own way and doing things your way. This reasoning breaks my heart. If you are in defiance of the law, you are in defiance of God. It's that simple, and that humbling. This is the most dangerous reason for not obeying the law. Not only is it not a good testimony to other homeschoolers or your own children, but it makes your defense in a court of law quite difficult! Choose to submit instead. God will bless your obedience. And it's His blessing we want, not the curse!

WHEN YOU NEED HELP

There may come a time, despite your good intentions, that you need legal representation or advice. The Homeschool Legal Defense Association (HSLDA) can do just that. However, you must be a current member of the association, and there is a hefty membership fee. If you think you are in a position that may be threatened—that is, if you have had problems with the state or district before, if your area/state is notorious for hounding homeschoolers, or if you just want the peace of mind of knowing you are protected—it would be advisable to join HSLDA. However, a cautionary note is in order here. Do not just "do your own thing" because you know the HSLDA will represent you if you get caught! That is sinning intentionally so grace will abound. As Paul said, "God forbid!" (Romans 6:2, KJV).

WHY YOU SHOULD OBEY

What should our motivation be for obedience? Should we do it out of fear of what the state will do if we don't? Should we do it so we look good to others? Should we do it only because it is the right thing to do? These are all worldly reasons why we should obey. God's reasons reach further and deeper.

Positive Results of Obedience

Observe and hear all these words which I command thee, that it may go well with thee, and with thy children after thee for ever, when thou doest that which is good and right in the sight of the LORD thy God.
—DEUTERONOMY 12:28, KJV

When a man's ways please the LORD, he maketh even his enemies to be at peace with him.
—PROVERBS 16:7, KJV

Fear none of those things which thou shalt suffer: behold, the devil shall cast some of you into prison, that ye may be tried; and ye shall have tribulation ten days: be thou faithful unto death, and I will give thee a crown of life.

—REVELATION 2:10, KJV

Negative Results of Disobedience

And the LORD said unto Moses, Whosoever hath sinned against me, him will I blot out of my book.

—EXODUS 32:33, KJV

Because he hath despised the word of the LORD, and hath broken his commandment, that soul shall utterly be cut off; his iniquity shall be upon him.

—NUMBERS 15:31, KJV

Then shall they call upon me, but I will not answer; they shall seek me early, but they shall not find me: For that they hated knowledge, and did not choose the fear of the LORD: they would none of my counsel: they despised all my reproof.

—PROVERBS 1:28-30, KJV

God is serious about obedience! The rewards are great, and the punishments are devastating, and both are eternal. Is it your intent to obey the authorities God has placed in your life? Do you have a heart of obedience? Whatever your heart is, you can be sure your children have seen it and will emulate it.

 MARGIE

I admit that the reason we decided to homeschool was a flat-out rejection of the public school system. My twins started out in public school, and within months both were diagnosed with one problem or another. The school's offer of help felt more like an intrusion to me. My kids never finished one full year in public school. At that point I wanted nothing to do with public education or any government agency for that matter.

Because of my husband's job situation we traveled quite a bit. We were never in one place for more than six to eight months. Thank God we were homeschooling! Otherwise the twins never would have experienced any level of continuity in their lives. Unfortunately, because of this constant uprooting, I neglected to ever let anyone know we were homeschoolers—legally. The funny thing is, no one seemed to notice. I was relieved because I didn't want the state in my business anyway.

Finally after four years of moving from district to district and even state to state, my husband found a job he could keep. We actually stayed in one place for an entire year! We found a good church and for the first time in as long as I could remember, we made friends! There was a homeschool support group at our church, and I enthusiastically joined it. We had a different speaker every month. One month we had our state's homeschool lobbyist visit and talk to us about how hard she was working to improve the legislation with regard to homeschooling. It was there that I first realized my failing.

The lobbyist only had one complaint directed at her own people: Stand up and be counted! We were making her job a lot harder by hiding. How could she convince legislators that we had needs when our numbers seemed so small? Why would the governor loosen the reins on homeschoolers when many of them weren't following the laws that were already in place? That made homeschooling look like an underground movement instead of the mainstream movement it was in reality. And it made us look bad!

I sat there knowing that I was one of those homeschoolers hiding from the state. I now knew it affected more than just me. It affected all homeschoolers in our state. I felt terrible. The very next day I went to our local school district office and filed as a homeschooler. To my pleasant surprise, all that happened was that the nice lady at the counter took my letter of intent and filed it with all the others. No questions asked. No reprimand. Actually, no attention whatsoever! Maybe one person doesn't make a difference, but I felt better about it—and I can only be accountable for myself.

FOR MORE INFORMATION ON THIS TOPIC

The Ultimate Guide to Homeschooling by Debra Bell (Tommy Nelson, 1997).
Homeschooling Almanac 2000—2001 by Mary and Michael Leppert (Prima Publishing, 1999).

COUNT THE COST/REAP THE JOY

Good citizenship is not just something we teach through a ninth-grade civics class. It's something we live each and every day. We model it for our children, and they in turn learn which rules are worth obeying and which are not (the latter being only those that require us to disobey the clear commands of God).

Have you investigated the homeschool rules of your state and district? If not, do so soon, even today. Choose to walk in obedience and not in defiance.

Write down or discover the answer to these questions:

1. What category of regulations are homeschoolers in your state under—low, moderate, or high?

_____

_____

_____

_____

2. What are the specific requirements for homeschoolers in your state?

_____

_____

_____

_____

3. Have you adhered to each requirement to the satisfaction of the state?

_____

_____

_____

_____

4. What, if any, requirement is a particular challenge to your own will? How will you submit to it in the spirit God expects?

_____

_____

_____

5. What do you want your children to learn from your example?

_____

_____

_____

How Should I Plan?

WHEN BEGINNING A long journey, it is important to plan your itinerary. We do this for a variety of reasons. We want to have some idea of what it will take to get to our destination. Where will we be at the end of each day? Will our chosen route get us where we want to go, and will it get us there on time? If we get detoured, can we rely on our carefully planned map to get back on track? And finally, if we need to tell someone else where to find us, can they follow our directions?

Planning is more than knowing how to write lesson plans. Planning supports you on your journey and helps both you and your children stay focused on the destination. There's nothing wrong with stopping somewhere unexpectedly for a while to enjoy the view. There's nothing wrong with taking side trips, as long as you eventually get back on the main road. Otherwise you won't get where you want to go. Do you and your children know where you're going in your homeschooling?

PICKING DESTINATIONS—GOAL SETTING

What is your destination? Sometimes it is chosen for you—for example, when you go on a business trip. Sometimes it is a vacation. Sometimes it is a family reunion. Sometimes it is a deliberate move in search of a different and better lifestyle. The reasons driving your trip may be many or there may be only one. Goals are the destinations of your homeschool journey. To quote Microsoft®, "Where do you want to go today?"

Consider three types of goals for your children and yourself:

• *Academic goals—what you want to do.* These are what you would expect them to be. They are specific, measurable, attainable goals. You may even choose one or more for yourself (i.e., I will learn algebra alongside my fourteen-year-old).

• *Process goals—how you do what you want to do.* These may target study habits, writing skills, neatness, work quality, the ability to work independently, etc. They are just as important as academic goals. For yourself you might choose something like "To organize our materials prior to the next day."

• *Spiritual goals—why you do what you do.* These goals target biblical principles that lead to success. Our children must learn obedience, to work heartily as unto the Lord, to focus on things above, etc. These are life principles that directly affect our attitudes about what we do. Check your own spiritual journey. Where are you on your walk with God?

SAMPLE GOALS

Academic goals (what they do):
CHOOSE GOALS THAT TARGET SPECIFIC ACADEMIC CONCEPTS.

1. Jason will learn to write in cursive by the end of this year.
2. Colleen will learn her multiplication tables with 90 percent accuracy.
3. John will learn the elements of the periodic table with 95 percent accuracy.
4. Kayla will be able to recite Psalm 23 with 100 percent accuracy.

Process goals (how they do it):
USE ADVERBS THAT SHOW HOW THE ACADEMICS SHOULD BE DONE.

1. Jason will be able to write all required work neatly.
2. Colleen will be able to work independently during math.
3. John will be able to finish his required reading completely each week.
4. Kayla will be able to use a variety of sources to research her project.

Spiritual goals (with what attitude do they do it):
USE BIBLICAL EXPECTATIONS FOR EVERYDAY SITUATIONS.

1. Jason will patiently read to his brother.
2. Colleen will humbly accept praise for her good work.
3. John will lovingly respond to his younger sister.
4. Kayla will apologize quickly when she has wronged her sister.

Goals can be both final destinations and mile markers. The ultimate goal is to have success as God defines success. If we have success, we will bring glory to God in all that we say and do. As mile markers, goals guide us along the way to our final destination. They must be clearly posted and understandable. We should know what we can expect when we get there.

CHOOSING APPROPRIATE ROUTES—CURRICULUM CHOICES

To reach one destination there may be a variety of routes. Some are more direct than others. It depends upon how quickly you need to get there. It can also depend upon whether or not you have money to stay overnight somewhere or even have enough gas. Curriculum choices are like alternative routes on a road map. You can figure it out yourself, but that can be risky if you have never gone to this particular destination before. You might ask AAA® to prepare an itinerary for you that would illuminate the most direct routes with the fewest delays or detours. Or you might ask someone who's been there before which routes they prefer and what, if any, problems they experienced along the way. The final option is to just drive where the wind leads you, hoping you arrive eventually.

There are many curriculum choices available to homeschoolers today, more than ever before. The choices can be dizzying. Practically, the best advice is to look at your goals and match curricula or resources based upon whether or not they will help your child reach those goals. A particular prepackaged curriculum may not be suitable. It may address some goals but totally ignore others. Take your time, and plan carefully. Ask other homeschoolers who have similar goals for their children what they used. Preview materials when possible. At this time the only secure way to do that is to attend a homeschool convention and leisurely stroll the exhibit hall. Ordering directly from a catalog is risky and may cost you more. You risk accumulating a pile of materials that you'll never use and hoping you can get some money back at a used curriculum sale. Many companies offer a "try before you buy" option so you can preview their materials through a demo or sample materials.

As you match each goal with appropriate curriculum choices, some choices may address more than one goal. Just remember that one size does *not* fit all. Be willing to find the right size for your child. If not, it's like wearing the wrong size shoes; they pinch from being too tight, or they rub from being too large. Either way, it hurts and you are wasting money.

THE ROAD MAP—LESSON PLANNING

Different homeschool philosophies address the issue of lesson planning differently. A surprising number of homeschoolers do not even write lesson plans. As a former teacher I have never understood this decision. For some it may be a deliberate omission, but for many others it is a matter of ignorance. They don't know why or how they should prepare lesson plans.

Why?

Maybe your state requires homeschoolers to turn in their lesson plans; maybe it doesn't. But satisfaction comes from the process of preparing them. As a teacher I only had one principal who required his teachers to turn in their lesson plans each week. Yes, it kept me on my toes, but it also made sure I was prepared to teach each week. When I worked for principals who were not as stringent, I still prepared my lesson plans, more for my own sanity and security than for him. It was a matter of taking the time to thoroughly plan for my students. It showed that I cared. It also showed that I was serious about my job.

Your children deserve the time that it takes to prepare their school experiences. Many avoid this task because they are intimidated by it. Not a former teacher? Join the club! Why should you prepare your lessons? Because your children's education deserves to be taken seriously. Because it saves time in the long run. Because it shows your dedication as a teacher and your love as a parent. The reasons for not preparing lesson plans do not stand up to scrutiny.

How?

Even as a teacher I was frustrated with lesson plan books. There doesn't seem to be one on the market that meets every teacher's planning needs. So I always do the best I can with what I have to work with. I could include a sample lesson plan sheet in the appendix of this book, but it would only address the needs of a fraction of homeschoolers. The best way is to create your own format. However you choose to create it, try to include the following elements:

- A week at a glance; a place for the date.
- A place to remark on each subject taught.
- A place to remark on the grade levels taught.
- A place to comment on how well or how much of the plan was accomplished.

Basically, that's all you need to include. Below is a sample from my own lesson plan book. I only teach two children, and it works well for me. I used a store-bought teacher lesson plan book.

GRADES TAUGHT: 2ND AND 4TH
WEEK BEGINNING: *Monday, March 20, 2000*

Quiet Time/Handwriting
AWANA study handbook
CAC-/Nn/day 1
CDC-/Qq/day 1

Reading

Silent Rdg. for 15 mins.
Junior Great Books story, 1ˢᵗ reading
Comprehension Lesson:
Context #4

Math

CDC-Lesson 75
CAC-Lesson 46

Science/History

Unit Study
"The Human Body"
vocabulary

Spelling/Latin/Grammar

CAC-Spelling Lesson 24; write words
CDC-Latin Word Roots 111-120; look up first 5 words in English dictionary
Daily Oral Language

Writing/Journal

Journal Topic
"How could you encourage someone you love today?"
CAC-3 paragraphs
CDC-5 paragraphs

CDC = CHRISTOPHER
CAC = CHARLES

As you can see, I only write enough to remind me of what we hope to accomplish that particular day. You may find that you need to write more or less than I do. Whatever works for you is fine. We may not always get to everything on the plan. I check off things as we go. At the end of a week, I circle all the things that were not checked and rewrite them in the next week's plan, to keep us focused. That way, along our journey we won't miss an important exit!

SCENIC OVERLOOKS AND DETOURS—RETEACHING AND
ENRICHMENT

Sometimes along our journey we make a stop. Our children ask us
to take time out so we can take in incredible scenery, or they may
require us to take a detour off the beaten path. Many travelers
choose instead to stay on the main roads and speed past the scenic
overlooks, worried they may not make good time. But if your child
needs to make a pit stop . . .

In a classroom when a particularly interesting topic arises from
the text, a teacher is usually not inclined to further investigate that
topic. It would take too much time away from her scope and
sequence. But children benefit tremendously from the enrichment
gained from deep exploration of a topic. There is no reason as
homeschoolers not to take time to delve deeply into subjects that
your children find intriguing. The only time restraints you have,
you have probably put on yourself. *You* are in the driver's seat!
Digging deeper adds relevance to a study. It gives children the
opportunity to explore their interests and talents. It is a gift that they
have as homeschoolers.

Another reason you may decide to take a detour in your studies is that your child may require reteaching of a particular concept
or added practice with a certain skill. In a regular classroom he
would be left further and further behind, eventually having no hope
of catching up. Isn't it wonderful that you can give your child the
gift of time? You have to be willing to stop, check the map, and
choose an alternate route if necessary. You may have to teach your
child in a different style. You may have to choose a different curriculum. Maybe you just have to spend longer than the recommended time on a certain skill to get it up to par. The goal here is
mastery. The decision to stop and take a look around on your journey is driven by the needs of your children. It should not be driven
by your inner clock or scope and sequence.

Reaching Your Destination—Assessment and Evaluations

How do you know when you've reached your destination? There may be signs welcoming you. You may know by looking at your map that you've reached the end of your trip. You may even know you're there by the landmarks you now observe. Yet you must be sure you're in the right place or your journey is not really over. Does it look like you expected it to look? Your trip may not necessarily end with the traditional school year. In fact, it may continue deep into the summer. What matters is that you get where you intended to go.

Sharing Your Trip Photos—Portfolios

One of the most effective ways to communicate your child's progress is through portfolios. Not unlike an artist's portfolio, his or her best work is displayed. Other times it is a sampling of what your child can do. A portfolio can also chronicle a child's journey toward mastery. A portfolio should be enjoyable to share. It shouldn't be so full that those you share it with have to hide their yawns. Choosing what goes into a portfolio and how often you place items into it are key.

We keep our photos in a variety of formats, and our children's portfolios can be just as versatile. Let's discuss three common ways to keep a portfolio and their advantages and disadvantages:

The Shoebox Method

This is probably the easiest portfolio to keep. Just as the name describes, a container of some kind is used to house everything you've chosen to keep for your child. No matter how attractively simple this method appears, it is flawed in more than one way. Yes, you get points for keeping your child's work at all. However, it is difficult to find particular items, and this method tempts you to keep *everything*! Can you organize the shoebox method so it is user-friendly? Yes. You can divide the container into sections by subject or grade. Is it the most effective way to maintain a portfolio? Not by a long shot!

The Digital Method

This is the newest portfolio method to hit town. For those who are technology-driven, this method appeals to your sense of creativity and fun. By using your computer, scanner, the Internet, your video camera, digital camera, etc., you can create a spectacular display of what your child learned this year. With CD burners becoming more and more affordable, the digital portfolio's day has come. You can keep a record of anything you want on CD without fear of degradation. However, as much fun as this method is, it is also quite time-consuming. If you do not already have all the equipment you'd like to use, it also becomes an expensive choice.

Even if you choose one of the other portfolio methods, you can choose to digitally store some of your child's experiences. Take pictures on a field trip with a digital camera, and insert them into your child's written reflection of that trip. Make a videotape of your child competing in your district's speech contest or of him explaining how he created a time-consuming project. The possibilities are endless!

The Artist's Portfolio Method

This method combines the creativity of the digital method with the relative ease of the shoebox method. It requires organization without sacrificing fun! All you need is a three-ring binder for each child. Divide this binder by however many topics you teach. Then once a week (preferably on Fridays) help your child sort his work from the week into the binder. I suggest that only the best work be kept in your portfolio. So tests, final drafts of a report, field trip reflections, etc., go into it. You may choose to do one of two things with the remaining papers. You can throw them away, or you can maintain them in file folders according to topic. The key is to make this a regular part of your week. When work is completed for the week, take a few moments to sort it into the portfolio. Over the course of a year you will be able to look back at what your child's best work was in

August and what it was in May. You can incorporate digital technology into this portfolio. Using clear plastic sleeves, include a disc or scanned photos showcasing special accomplishments.

Whichever of these methods you use, sharing your child's portfolio is the best part. Just as we love to show off our photos from our vacations, we love to show off our children's portfolios. Take time out at least twice a year to invite family and friends over for a portfolio party. Serve refreshments, dress up, and allow your child to show what he or she has learned this year. If he or she took part in creating his or her portfolio, he or she will expertly communicate all that it shows.

Beginning to maintain a portfolio early will pay off later when college is looming. Many colleges and universities accept portfolios from homeschoolers for admission. Start now; don't wait!

DID YOU ENJOY YOUR TRIP? SELF-REFLECTION AND JOURNALING

Journaling is a powerful tool, providing students with the opportunity to express themselves and improve their written communication. It also provides parents with needed insight into their teaching and their child's learning. Used in conjunction with portfolios, a journal of your and your children's self-reflections can help you see more clearly where you've come from. That way you can keenly see where you're going as well. One caution is not to make a journal a mandatory, graded activity. Our children must improve their written communication by becoming fluent and flexible writers; however, it should not become a chore. And yet the more they do it, the better at it they will become.

 **MICHAEL**

I wanted my two girls homeschooled because I wanted my wife and I to have the greatest impact on building our children's character. There were several families from our church who were already homeschooling whom I admired. Although my children were attending a Christian school, the children who attended the school came from a variety of backgrounds. I appreciated the fact that the families from our church who homeschooled were like-minded in the values they taught to their children.

Well, we just finished our first year of homeschooling. Kelly is nine years old, and Mikaela is eight. Although I wanted Diane to homeschool from the very beginning, she wasn't ready. However, we both became concerned about the influences our girls were picking up from other children at school and from the neighborhood, and so Diane was determined to give it a try. As we both focused on working on the girls' character, God was busy working on ours. As the year progressed, God not only worked mightily in our children's lives, but in our own.

The many blessings we have shared as a family because of homeschooling have confirmed in both our hearts that we made the right decision. The evenings were spent together as a family instead of running around, rushing dinner to get the homework done and the kids to bed. Schoolwork was done during the day, and it was fun and educational. Day-to-day situations became opportunities to teach. Although the majority of the teaching falls upon my wife, I had the girls each Wednesday afternoon so Diane could have some personal time. I also read with the girls each night while Diane prepared lessons for the next day. That made it a family affair. Although Diane began the year with great apprehension, we have seen God's hand in our lives, and Diane has already planned out next year's lessons. My kids will tell you homeschool is cool, and so do I. I have found that in the tapestry of life, which God has woven with His own hand, He has brought our family closer together, that we might love and encourage one another even more.

FOR MORE INFORMATION ON THIS TOPIC

The Homeschooling Father by Michael Farris (Loyal Publishing, 1999).

The Successful Homeschool Family Handbook by Dr. Raymond Moore (Thomas Nelson, 1994).

COUNT THE COST/REAP THE JOY

Goals are the gas that fuels your homeschool and drives you forward. Consider the chart below, and create one of your own as a road map.

	Written Goal	**Curricula Used to Meet Goal**
Academic Goal 1		
Academic Goal 2		
Academic Goal 3		
Process Goal 1		
Process Goal 2		
Process Goal 3		
Personal Goal 1		
Personal Goal 2		
Personal Goal 3		
Spiritual Goal 1		
Spiritual Goal 2		
Spiritual Goal 3		

Statement of Commitment:

What Should I Teach?

FOR MANY OF US, the easiest way to answer this question is to teach exactly what the public or private school teaches. Yet the easiest way is not always the best. Even if you've pulled your child home to school midyear, you can still have the liberating experience of choosing what you want your children to learn. Back in Chapter One you were asked to write down your philosophy of education. It's time to revisit your answer. What you believe education is all about will lead you to what to teach. Within that framework are a variety of approaches that become the *how* for what you will teach.

YOUR PHILOSOPHY OF EDUCATION

Every teacher has his or her own philosophy of education, including you. That is, what do you believe is the purpose of education? The answers vary depending upon three factors: a teacher's own educational experience, his or her deeply rooted beliefs, and what he or she learned in college about education. Most homeschoolers have the advantage of not having gone through a teacher training program; so their philosophy of education is based primarily on the first two mentioned sources.

Your own educational experience as a child weighs heavily here. Those who had very positive school experiences want to duplicate that experience for their children. Conversely, those who had extremely negative school experiences will do whatever it takes to avoid that experience for their own children. However, both are reactionary approaches and should not be the sole consideration.

Your philosophy, as a Christian, should be based primarily upon what you believe and know to be true. You have all the spiritual truth you need in the revealed Word of God. There is a difference between the pursuit of knowledge and the pursuit of wisdom, and God wants to reveal the difference to you personally if you do not yet know it. If you are not sure which God values most, do a word study on both *knowledge* and *wisdom* and see where God leads you. What the Word reveals to you will shape your philosophy of education according to God's truth.

Below are four common educational philosophies to which homeschoolers subscribe.

• *Education is for learning the three R's; back to the basics; college preparation.* This philosophy is a knee-jerk reaction to the failing of the public schools to support the basics. Parents are tired of their children not knowing how to spell or how to write a complete sentence or still struggling with their multiplication tables. The embarrassing lack of history and geography knowledge has made Americans the laughingstock of the world! These parents see the objectives of their job as home educators quite clearly. Their philosophy is skill-oriented and textbook-driven.

• *Education is for preparing students to become contributing members of society.* This philosophy is both proactive and reactive. Traditionally, public education has claimed this philosophy for itself as a whole. Ignorance does not help drive an economy. It does not better society. Yet our current state reflects graduating high schoolers lacking the skills they need to qualify for entry-level positions in business. And the business community is screaming mad! They're not kidding when they say, "It's hard to find good help these days." That is more true now than ever before. Homeschoolers who operate under this philosophy provide their children with a multitude of real-life experiences. Some own and operate their own family businesses, within which their children are participants. Apprenticeships are appealing to this philosophy. Young men are prepared to support a family, and young women are prepared for the traditional role of homemaker.

College is not discouraged, but starting your own business is considered just as valid a choice.

• *Education is for the purpose of learning about the world through God's eyes.* This philosophy is lived out almost exclusively through the Scriptures. Most academic subjects are taught via the Bible. Character study is the core curriculum. Preparation for college or career is a secondary concern. Attending Bible college following the high school years is the natural order of education. Again traditional roles of men and women are reinforced.

• *Education is the process of learning about life from experience.* This philosophy spurs on a very relevant yet unstructured learning environment. Whether a family lives on a farm in the country or in a high-rise in the city, street smarts are valued. What God has to teach us about life is all around us, in our own lives and the lives of others. It's just a matter of observation and involvement in the lives of others. These are very community-minded families who strive to learn all they can from within so they can give to those without.

A COMBINED PHILOSOPHY

Fortunately, life is bigger than any one philosophy. If you desire a balanced approach, it is more likely that your philosophy is a combination of two or more of the above-mentioned philosophies. The idea is to be open to the unique needs of your own family. No one way is right. God made us all different with different needs and desires. Make sure you look at the big picture. Try not to get caught up in someone else's idea of the *right* way to teach.

HOW SHOULD I TEACH IT?

Just as there is no one right way to look at education, there is no one right way to teach. The following approaches are representative of homeschooling in today's society. Rest assured that ten years from now there will be more ways to teach—technology assures that. Each approach has its advantages and disadvantages. Over the course of your homeschooling career, you may use more than one of these approaches.

Prescripted Curriculum (School in a Box)

Textbook publishers offer whole grade curricula to homeschoolers at significantly lower prices since we are not buying classroom sets. Many companies, such as Bob Jones University, offer testing services as well. They are full-service curricula providers. The attraction, especially to a beginning homeschooler, is that everything from Bible to science is laid out in an easy to follow format. For "school at home" homeschoolers, this approach is exactly what they're looking for. It is textbook/workbook-driven, tests and answer keys are included, and they feel secure under the umbrella of a traditional approach.

Even though purchasing this curriculum is usually cheaper for homeschoolers, it may still be cost-prohibitive for many. After all, multiply approximately $250 by four children and you can see the problem. Used curriculum sales through your local homeschool support group is one of the most cost-effective ways to obtain this curriculum. You may think of it as an investment because all of your children will eventually use it. However, many homeschoolers discover, much to their dismay, that not all of their children benefit from the same type of curriculum approach.

The Unit Study Approach

This approach has become increasingly popular. It consists primarily of a topical study that then integrates the varying subject areas. For example, a unit study on flight would include literature on flight, scientific principles of flight, art projects on flight, historical perspectives about flight, etc. The beauty of this approach is that you can adjust the experiences according to each child's level, so that the whole family studies the same thing. A growing number of homeschool vendors are carrying unit studies in their catalogs. Night Owl is one of them. Valerie Bendt, well-known homeschool author, has written a book for parents about creating unit studies themselves.

This approach is interest-driven, using a variety of sources and materials to teach necessary concepts.

However, there is a danger of holes in a child's learning. Specific skills still must be taught and mastered. Learning about bats is wonderfully exciting but becomes trivial if the child cannot communicate what he has learned through writing or speaking.

The Unschooling Approach

The subtitle of *The Unschooling Handbook* by Mary Griffith (Prima Publishing, 1998) is "How to Use the Whole World as Your Child's Classroom." This describes the unschooling approach. It is not traditional. It is not replicating "school at home." The essence of unschooling is that there is no magic formula, no simple solution-in-a-box for every child's educational problem. Unschooling is simply a way to tailor learning to the specific needs of each child and each family. This approach ultimately puts children in charge of their own educations. There are few to no curricula, lesson plans, schedules, or scope and sequence. It is learner-directed, seeking out mentors or facilitators when necessary. For the beginning homeschooler who is used to the concept of "school," this approach may be intimidating. It does, however, provide both parents and children the freedom they each need to be as diverse in their learning as possible.

The Eclectic Approach

As previously mentioned, there is not one right way to teach anyone anything. We are all different and learn differently. God has graciously given us a myriad of ways to teach our children. Jesus Himself, the Master Teacher, used more than a lecture format to teach both His disciples and the multitudes. You have many strategies and approaches from which to choose. Remember these three attributes to good teaching: fluency, flexibility, and originality. *Fluency* means teaching in a way and a language your children will understand. *Flexibility* means to think of as many ways as possible to solve a problem or teach a skill. *Originality* speaks to customizing the material to the individual learner, possibly in ways never tried before on that child. Don't use particular curricula or strategies just because that's all you know. Expand your horizons. As a teacher you must always be on the hunt for new ways to meet the learning needs of your children. If not, they might be better off in a traditional school.

HOW MUCH SHOULD I TEACH?

Should I teach for two or six hours per day? Should I spend more time on math or on reading? Should we do school all year or stop during the summer? Isn't it important that we finish the whole book? These questions and many, many more indicate two things. One: most parents are utterly confused as to the expectations of homeschoolers. Two: they show how seriously homeschooling parents take their chosen responsibility. Let's deal with some of these questions and then encourage you in the decision-making power that is ultimately yours.

Should I teach for two or six hours per day? How many hours per day to teach may be dictated by your state or district. If you are also required to log those hours, most likely your district has provided you with a way to do that. However, across the country this requirement is changing for the better. Schools realize that by their own admission, the amount of real teaching/learning time that occurs in school is much less than the time they actually spend at school. Special activities such as music, art, or physical education take up a lot of time. Pullout programs such as health or drug education or counseling also take a bite out of the school day. Disruptions caused by students entering and leaving a classroom in order to receive special education also cut into a teacher's precious time with her students. Then there's getting settled before first class and before and after lunch and getting ready to leave for the day, not to mention discipline problems. You do not have to deal with any of the stresses and struggles a classroom teacher does. So use your God-given time wisely. Take as much or as little time as your child needs in order to master his work. There's no need to rush through anything.

Should we spend more time on math or reading? This question, like so many of the others, begins with the word *should*. There are no *shoulds* in homeschooling. What does your child need to know? Teach it! Long-term homeschoolers say that over time they will learn it all, just not all of it every year. This again depends on what your philosophy of education includes. If your child is college-bound, certain requirements will be made of him, and it is your job to spend time on those things. Some children are just not ready to spend an hour a day on writing. They may not be ready physically or mentally for certain other tasks as well. That's fine. Give them what they need when they need it.

Should we do school all year or stop during the summer? Another *should*. Keep in mind that certain districts do require homeschoolers to teach a certain number of days per year. The traditional school year is between 170 to 180 days long. At most that is six months per year! You can do better than that. It is common knowledge that approximately six weeks at the beginning of each school year is devoted to review because of skill loss over the summer. Many areas are experimenting with year-round schools. Many of these have failed due to the traditional vacation times. Many parents would love to go on a family vacation when it is better for them to be away from work and not just when there is a scheduled school break, but they have no choice. You do. My family does school in some way all year round. Math especially suffers if we do not. Silent reading is daily all year long. Written reflections on any trips we take are also common. Sometimes we use the summer to tackle an interesting unit study that we just didn't have time to do during the "regular" school year. Again, do what you want when you want. That's part of the beauty of it all.

Is it important that we finish the whole book? Conversely, *is it okay if my son finishes his book early?* These issues about scope and sequence are basically inconsequential for the homeschooler. I have one child who always finishes everything early and one who finishes on time or late. *Early* and *late* are terms that apply to a traditional school situation. Since most of us have been indoctrinated into that environment, it is sometimes hard to escape it. However, there are instances when completion within a prescribed time frame is necessary.

Scope and sequence are terms used often by education and curriculum writers. For example, textbook companies write their math, science, language arts, and reading texts with a traditional school year in mind. If you are using one of the prescripted curricula, they will present a scope and sequence chart in the teacher's manual to help you gauge your progression through the material. The danger here is that you will panic if your child does not progress normally. For example, it is the end of May and your son still has forty math lessons to complete! First, ask yourself, "What is the worst thing that will happen if he doesn't finish by June 10?" Answer: He will have to continue until he does finish. Is this a problem? I hope not! That's the beauty of homeschooling—our children can progress at their own rates. That is a gift—the gift of time! And if they finish early, the same thinking applies—it's not a problem. He or she can just continue on to the next level if you wish.

It's difficult not to ask other homeschoolers, "What lesson are you on?" especially if you are using the same curriculum. Yet this can be detrimental. Any time we compare our children's development or progress to another's, it only causes trouble. God would not have you keep account or measure yourselves by man's standards. This is a good place to practice biblical principles and to teach them to your children.

Sometimes there are situations that require us to stick within a time restraint—for example, completion of specific coursework leading to college entrance, or prerequisite coursework during the high school years. It is important in specific instances to familiarize yourself with the requirements and then meet or even exceed them. Just be aware that if your child is not ready, he's not ready! This is not the time to push him into a box he is not ready to handle. Set your child up for success by planning ahead.

One of the most impressive characteristics of homeschoolers is their dedication to ensuring a quality education for their children. The commitment is real and solid. In our attempts to make sure our children get what they need, we sometimes fall prey to traditional school thinking that says there is only one right way or there is a "best" way to do things. Remember, God made your child different from any other, and therefore his or her needs may be different as well. You can use different approaches within different time frames with each child. To do otherwise is like trying to force a square peg into a round hole. Instead of trying to change the peg into another shape, find the right hole!

JEANNINE

We were extremely happy with the "education" our children were getting at our private Christian school. I was always amazed at all they were being taught, things I didn't learn at their ages. However, the amount of homework times for three kids was staggering and robbed us of our family life. I understand that in order to teach the kids at the higher level, it was necessary for the kids to do work at home, but I just wanted more time for our family. I wanted to be able to sit down in the evenings and watch TV together or read a book, play soccer, basketball, or whatever sport without our schoolwork suffering. I remember when I asked friends how homeschooling was going, they told me all of the pluses, including more family time. After 2:00 P.M. you're on your own . . . whatever your family wants to do. They told me how they had gone down to the beach, etc., and that appealed to me.

That has also been the most wonderful blessing for us since we have been homeschooling. In the evenings we have read books together, watched TV, and even gone to the beach. Our oldest son is playing soccer for the first time ever because we could never balance two games per week with homework. Our oldest daughter is on the city swim team. She wanted to join a year ago, but there was no way she could practice three to four times per week and still do her homework. So homeschooling has really opened up our lives and allows us to enjoy life so much more now.

Pulling the kids out in the middle of the year was actually comforting to me. I figured they were already in the swing of things, and I also figured I couldn't mess up too bad in half a year. It was just a half of a school year commitment, so if it didn't go well, they could go back to "school" in the fall. So pulling them out halfway through the school year made more sense to me. I would have been more scared beginning in September and looking at nine months!

God has played such a big part in this decision. I have had such peace from Him, and I feel He is pleased that we are living a much calmer, quieter life. "Make it your ambition to lead a quiet life, to mind your own business and to work with your hands, just as we told you" (1 Thessalonians 4:11, NIV). I love teaching the children the Bible. Our attempts at family devotions always stopped after four or five days in the past because we would be running late, etc. This way our devotions are built right into our day!

FOR MORE INFORMATION ON THIS TOPIC

The Unschooling Handbook by Mary Griffith (Prima Publishing, 1998).
The Homeschool Manual by Theodore E. Wade, Jr. (Gazelle, 1998).

COUNT THE COST/REAP THE JOY

Using a concordance, Bible dictionary, and regular dictionaries, look up *wisdom*. Then answer the following questions:

1. List synonyms and antonyms for this word or quality.

_____

_____

_____

2. Identify related words from the same root.

_____

_____

_____

_____

3. Look up at least three Scripture references using this word. List and summarize them here.

_____

_____

_____

4. Consider:

How do I see this quality in God?

_____

_____

_____

Why is it important to God, others, and myself?

_____

_____

_____

How is it cultivated?

_____

_____

_____

How is it hindered?

_____

_____

_____

What biblical character shows me what this quality looks like in real life?

_____

_____

_____

5. Rewrite a new definition based on your study.

_____

_____

_____

6. Rewrite your philosophy of education based on your study.

_____

_____

_____

7. Choose and memorize a key verse. Write it out here, with the reference.

_____

_____

_____

How Can I Organize
Our Homeschool?

ORGANIZATION IS MORE than a state of mind—it's a matter of the heart. There are a multitude of reasons why it is better to be more organized than not as homeschoolers. Some you're already familiar with, some you are not. The best way to approach anything is always God's way, and our God is a God of order and purpose. He does nothing haphazardly or by chance. Everything is planned and purposeful. Organization is a choice we make each and every day.

WHY BE ORGANIZED?

A discussion of disorganization illustrates the answer to this question in a powerful way. Below are six negative results associated with disorganization.

• *It leads to disorder.* You know when you live in the midst of disorder! It is not only uncomfortable for yourself but for anyone else who wanders into your surroundings.

• *It creates chaos.* Disorder leads to chaos. Chaos is defined as "utter confusion and disorder." God created the universe in an orderly and purposeful way. Your home and school environment is your universe, one you can choose to frame with order and purpose as well.

• *It causes stress.* Chaos brings stress, but creating order in your homeschool will alleviate unnecessary and harmful stress.

• *It implies you don't have your home and school all together.* What would you think if you walked into a traditional classroom and it was completely cluttered and disorganized or if, when asked where a particular child's work was, the teacher was unable to put her finger on it? That would communicate a lack of care and concern on the part of the teacher. It would *not* instill confidence.

• *It makes you inefficient.* The word *efficient* means "producing or capable of producing a desired effect with a minimum of effort or waste." In order for you and your children to be efficient workers or learners, you must all first desire to do things to your best effort and to do it with the least amount of effort or waste. Creating order will result in efficient workers.

• *It conveys you're not productive.* If one is productive, he or she produces abundantly and has favorable, useful, or positive results. If you want your children to give priority to their studies, you must first show them that it is a priority to you by your planning.

A disdain for negative consequences motivates us to make changes in our lifestyles. However, as true to life as these consequences may be, they do not address the heart of the matter. We need to go beyond following the letter of the law and embrace the spirit of the law. The Pharisees loved God's Law and followed it to the letter, believing that following the Law pleases God and brings peace. Yet their reliance on a step-by-step approach to heaven did not please God. It wasn't until He sent His Son, promoting the spirit of the Law, that real change could occur. Similarly, an insistence on the externals without building right heart motives in our homeschool is not what God desires.

A BIBLICAL PERSPECTIVE ON ORGANIZATION

Why be organized? Because if you desire to become more Christlike, you will desire orderliness. "But everything should be done in a fitting and orderly way" (1 Corinthians 14:40, NIV).

Sound impossible? It is if you try to do it in your own strength without relying on the Holy Spirit. But God knows your strengths and weaknesses. After all, He made you. If organization is a weak area for you, rejoice! Here is where God can show and share His strength!

> *This is love for God: to obey his commands. And his commands are not burdensome, for everyone born of God overcomes the world. This is the victory that has overcome the world, even our faith.*
>
> —1 JOHN 5:3-4, NIV

So if God says to do all things decently and in order, then (1) this command is not burdensome, and (2) your faith will triumph. This is not mind over matter, but faith over matter!

HOW ORGANIZED ARE YOU?

Many people joke about being "organizationally challenged." What that really means is that they don't have a natural tendency to be orderly. Guess what? God is bigger than that! You may be organized to varying degrees and not realize it. Let's look at some types of organized people.

• *The organizationally challenged.* There are two types of people in this group—those who are comfortable in the midst of chaos, and those who desperately seek to be organized but have always failed. For those who are in the first group, I want to make you *uncomfortable* in the midst of chaos. To be organized is a choice, not a personality trait. God has already put inside of us all we need to become more like Him. If He is orderly and purposeful, we should aspire to become the same. For those who have repeatedly tried and failed at being more organized, most likely you've been trying in your own strength and have left God out of your pursuit of orderliness. You cannot change your nature without Him.

• *The wanna-be organized.* Wanna-be's have a strong desire to become organized, but sometimes for the wrong reasons. Maybe you feel a sense of duty to your children or husband to be organized. Or

maybe you look around, and it seems that everyone else is more organized than you. You want to be organized because you *should* be organized, and it's eating you up inside. These reasons fall short.

• *The well-intentioned organized.* You're normally an organized
person, but lately, because of some life change, your life and home
have been thrown into a chaotic whirlwind. Don't be discouraged;
you just need to ask for help.

• *The already well-organized.* You are most comfortable when life
is structured and orderly. Sometimes people even tease you about
your well-ordered habits. The caution here is to make sure that
organization or the pursuit of it has not become an idol in your life.
If you're obsessed with running the perfect home, the perfect family, and the perfect homeschool, it may be time to reevaluate your
priorities.

HELP FOR A MORE ORGANIZED HOMESCHOOL

Those who struggle with organization are drawn to books, articles,
and experts that offer tips on regaining order in your life. What you
do with those tips is what matters. Everyone has his or her own ideas
about the best ways to organize life, but the truth is that someone
else's system may not work in your life. How do you know if a tip
will work for you and your family? Measure it against whether or
not it will help you live a life that is pleasing in God's sight. Some
tips will grab you immediately, while others will repel you. Listen
to the still small voice of God for direction. Below I offer you *principles* to guide you in your choosing, not rigid tips.

Your space. The goal here is not square footage, but efficient use
and planning of the space you already have. I used to think I
needed a house big enough to have a separate school room when I
began homeschooling. I even prayed for it! We did end up with a
separate work area with shelves and the computer. However, after
only a month I found that it did not suit our needs. So we ended
up at the kitchen table. That may make some of you cringe. Yes,
that means we must set up and clear that area a couple of times a

day, but it is in proximity to where I spend most of my time during the day. I can't afford to be locked away in another room with the kids while the laundry, dishes, etc., are waiting. I just don't have that luxury. What is important is that our kitchen table is big enough to spread out and close enough so that while the kids are working independently, I can still do my chores and not worry about them getting off-track.

The space issue is huge in many families. The more children you have, the more it is an issue. This is connected to your philosophy of education as well as to your personality. If you are more the "school at home" type, you will desire a separate "school" area. If you are the unschooling type, you will integrate school and the space it takes up into your everyday activities and spaces. Read-aloud time may even occur in the bathtub! Whatever you choose, choose it because it fits your lifestyle and teaching style, not because of what anyone else says about how it should be.

Your time. How we spend our time is usually dictated by our priorities. And some days we spend more time on the things we enjoy than on the things we don't. You may not enjoy teaching school. That's not wrong. But not taking the time to prepare or spending your teaching time doing other things may be. If you feel you do not have the time you need to do the things you need to do, it's time to reevaluate. Homeschooling must be a priority in your life. Those of us who find ourselves running around all day and then complaining that the kids didn't get their work done must stop and reconfigure. It is easy to get too busy doing other things. But our children's education must come first. God will bless you with the time you need to accomplish things if you do them His way. Let's look at God's priorities.

• *Time with and for God.* Time spent in communion with God in worship, in fellowship, in study, and in furthering His kingdom. Homeschooling can prepare your children to serve Him.

• *Time with and for family.* Time spent meeting your family's emotional, physical, and spiritual needs. Homeschooling can help here as well.

• *Time with and for your home.* Time spent in stewardship of the home God has provided for you and your family.

• *Time with and for friends.* Time spent in fellowship and hospitality. Time spent encouraging and counseling.

• *Time with and for individual pursuits.* Time spent on personal interests, sports, entertainment, or side businesses.

As you can see, in homeschooling time is a top priority. How you schedule your day is up to you. But if you have trouble getting everything done, most likely your priorities need adjusting.

Your supplies and materials. Maintaining the vast amounts of supplies and materials a homeschooler accumulates is a challenge. First, there is the issue of space. Second, the issue of what to keep. Most of us don't have the luxury of homeschooling in a separate room with cabinets and shelving. We're left with spaces that must be dual-purpose—a kitchen table, a dining room space, or the floor of our living room. Regardless of how much or how little space we have, we all have stuff to keep organized. Daily supplies can be kept in baskets or bins that are portable. Office supplies such as pencils, glue, paper, and art supplies might need a more permanent home. Wherever you choose to store them, they should be in reach and in sight. Otherwise you will forget that you have them and end up buying them all over again! You also want your children to learn how to put things away, and the best way to do that is to make it all accessible and visible. If we as parents are the only ones who know where things belong and how they should be put away, our children will never learn for themselves, and we will all be perpetually frustrated.

Your paperwork. The organization of paperwork is crucial. There are two types of paperwork you will encounter as a homeschooler: paperwork generated *by* your children and paperwork generated *for* your children. Why maintain any of it? What's wrong with putting it all in the "circular file" (the wastebasket)? First, it is difficult, if not impossible, to gauge children's progress if you don't keep account of what they have accomplished. Second, you may be required legally to maintain records of your homeschooling activities and progress by your state. In any case it is in your best interest to keep and organize any paperwork that has to do with homeschooling.

Paperwork generated by *your children.* You don't have to keep and file every piece of paper your child completes over the course of a school year. However, you should keep at least samples of your child's work. Choose a storage method that has easy insertion and removal. A three-ring binder is affordable and appropriate to store most work samples. Divide the binder by subject, and weekly insert their work samples. Train your children to do this themselves each Friday as a way to end the school week. Additional items such as artwork or three-dimensional projects can be stored in containers appropriate for their size. At the end of each year, have a box or similar container to store their binders, and label it by school year. Overall these suggestions are space-efficient and user-friendly. But only your consistency will make it work.

Paperwork generated for *your children.* Part of your job as a homeschooling parent is to maintain records for your district or state about your homeschool. This may include health records, birth certificates, testing results, lesson plans, attendance records, etc. Each child may require his or her own set of records. Whether you use a traditional filing system or an additional three-ring binder, it is important that you actually keep these records. Sometimes homeschoolers who have pulled their children out of the public sector tend to become isolationist and refuse to adhere to district or state guidelines relating to homeschooling. Christ said to "Give to Caesar what is Caesar's, and to God what is God's" (Matthew 22:21, NIV).

So if you are expected to file paperwork with the ruling authorities, you are biblically bound to do so. Maintain the records in a safe and organized manner. Be able to put your hands on them at a moment's notice. Your response to questions about your homeschool should not be made out of fear or bitterness. "Let your conversation be always full of grace, seasoned with salt, so that you may know how to answer everyone" (Colossians 4:6, NIV).

If you have the necessary documents, you can answer anyone in a way that is pleasing to God.

Your family. Organizing the lives of our family members is probably the most frustrating and difficult task. However, there are many negative connotations associated with this issue. "Running my life," "pulling the strings," "wrapped around her finger" are all phrases that conjure up images of a meddling parent or in-law. There's a difference between running a home and running someone's life. Keep this verse in mind when you consider orchestrating your family's lives: "Train a child in the way he should go: and when he is old, he will not depart from it" (Proverbs 22:6, KJV).

Consider first the implication of this verse. If you run your children's lives, they learn that someday as parents they should run *their* children's lives. Is that "the way he should go"? No. The *way* is God's way. The best way to set our children up to succeed as godly people and organized individuals is not by domineering them but by modeling it for them ourselves in our lives. Humbling? Hopefully so. Once when I was teaching a third-grade Sunday school class we discussed what it means to obey your parents. I gave the example that if a child's mom or dad asks him to clean his room, he should do it right away and without grumbling. One boy, normally quiet, spoke up. "But Mommy's room is always messy. Why do I have to keep mine clean?" Good question! If you want your children to be more organized, you must first become more organized yourself. They learn so much more by watching how we do things than by anything we say.

Becoming organized has more to do with your heart than with your storage capabilities. Whether or not you are naturally organized is beside the point. It is a choice, a decision we make each and every day for our own sake and the sake of our children. When you keep in mind that motivation, desiring to become more and more like our Lord, you will be empowered by the Holy Spirit to do what is pleasing in His sight. Our God is a God of order and purpose. Order promotes peace. And peace is from the Father. Take the time today to look at your life and see what God sees. Take the time to change disorder into order and therefore chaos into peace!

🍎 SHELLIE

It was the summer before our oldest son, Aaron, was to start kindergarten. I tried to prepare him for the idea of school by telling him what his days would be like. He listened attentively and was a little nervous but seemed to be excited as well.

Then we talked about his schedule. Aaron got very quiet and said, "Mom, I'll go to school in the morning and come home in the afternoon, right?"

"Yes," I said.

"Daddy will leave for work while I'm gone to school and come home late at night, right?"

"Yes."

"That means I won't get to see Daddy for five days."

We looked at each other. I hadn't thought of it quite like that before. Aaron and his daddy are exceptionally close. The thought of not seeing his daddy just wouldn't do.

"Mom, I don't want to go to kindergarten."

So began our journey as homeschoolers. Each year I think, *Next year we'll put our children in regular school.* So far God has said, "Not yet."

Each time I get to hug and kiss them in the middle of the day, each time I get to hear their laughter during a late breakfast, each time a single question about a Scripture turns into a half-hour conversation, I know we're doing the right thing for our family. Being the one who teaches them, sees their triumphs, and prays with them all day is very precious to me. Sharing my faith with them, singing together as we drive, and challenging them with questions about the personal character of God are priceless elements of many of my days.

My biggest concern is that I might forget what is important—that I might lose sight of why we decided to homeschool. Having time together as a family is of utmost importance to me and my husband. Because my husband is now in ministry work, his schedule varies. If our children attended "normal" school, there would be long periods of time that they wouldn't get "daddy days." Homeschooling gives us the opportunity to spend much more time together. Every Monday night during football season we make snacks, sit together on the floor with lots of pillows, and yell at the game. Sometimes the kids fall asleep on the floor beside us, and sometimes they don't. If we didn't homeschool, we'd lose our special Monday nights because they'd be doing their homework.

It's so easy to get burdened down with the workload and begin behaving like I wish I weren't doing this. I regularly do battle with the "Super Mom" mentality demon. And I often oscillate between thinking "we're doing great and will finish right on schedule" and "we'll never get through this year." Then I have to pray even more than usual. But I've discovered that God is using this process of homeschooling not just for my children, but for me as well. Seeing my weaknesses, facing my struggles, and fighting to be godly instead efficiently keeps me on my knees. And that's just where God wants me.

If ever God leads us to stop homeschooling, I want to look back on these years and know I gave all that I could, my very best, completely led and enabled by the Holy Spirit. The days and hours are so short. Twelve years in light of seventy isn't very much.

For More Information on This Topic

The Homeschool Manual by Theodore E. Wade, Jr. (Gazelle, 1998).

Emilie Barnes' 15 Minute Home and Family Organizer by Emilie Barnes (Inspirational Press, 1995).

Count the Cost/Reap the Joy

Whether you're a closet messy (one who hides his chaos) or a closet organizer (one who hides her obsession with neatness), you need peace. Most of us fall somewhere in between, but we all aspire to become more Christlike. Let's peek into those closets and under the bed . . .

1. Which disorganized area of your homeschool causes you the most stress?

_____

_____

_____

2. Why should it be more organized?

_____

_____

_____

3. Do your children's organizational habits frustrate you? Why?

_____

_____

_____

4. How would becoming more organized promote peace in your home?

_____

_____

_____

5. How would becoming more organized please God?

_____

_____

_____

PART III

CHARACTER AND COOPERATION

What End Results Should We Expect?

BIBLICAL PRINCIPLES EVEN apply to teaching one's own children. This chapter explores six competencies of successful learners and their biblical principles. These competencies can easily be turned into goals, but their greatest value lies in the fact that they are all directly connected to success in life. They are character issues. Homeschoolers have the distinct honor of building strong character in their children. You can build character through their work habits. First we must define, explore, and apply each competency. These describe *how* we do what we do.

A SELF-DIRECTED LEARNER

In order for a child to become a self-directed learner, he or she must accept responsibility for his or her own learning, be able to manage his or her own actions, and display integrity and honesty. A self-directed learner:

• *Knows what he needs.* This is an awareness that must be cultivated by you as his parent and teacher. Is he just going through the motions of school, or does he know where it leads?

• *Can take a personal inventory of strengths, likes, interests, and opinions.* The better we know ourselves, the better able we are to use our talents to achieve our goals.

• *States and supports personal points of view, even when his opinions are contrary to the ideas of others.* We want our children to be able to stand up for what they believe, especially when we are not around.

• *Designs an action plan to address an issue or problem of personal interest.* Can your child design a step-by-step plan to put into action a goal or solve a problem?

• *Demonstrates time management skills.* This is a skill you must model for your children. Do you wait until the last minute to do something? Or do you plan ahead, determining how long something even as simple as getting to church on time will take? Encourage your child to plan his or her time ahead as well.

• *Engages in self-reflection.* Journaling and periodic conferencing with your child will help him reflect on how he's doing and why he's doing what he's doing.

God's Word encourages active participation by His children. And sanctification demands it! Although I am usually leery of the word *self,* I invite you to explore it in this context. Self-control is one of the fruits of the Spirit (Galatians 5:22-23). It denotes the responsibility of each individual to yield to God. The child is accountable for his own learning. One day he will answer to God for his choices and actions. Encouraging children to take responsibility for their own education is a worthy goal. The danger lies in becoming self-sufficient in the process. Building responsibility along with dependence on God is key. "Yes, each of us will have to give a personal account to God" (Romans 14:12, NLT).

A PRODUCER OF QUALITY WORK

Quality assurance is highly valued in society. Why is it that quality is so elusive? It may be that differing expectations promote frustration and ambivalence. How can we communicate to children what we mean by quality? Awareness is half the battle.

What is *quality?* Quality means doing more than expected, going above and beyond the call of duty. We must encourage our children not to do just enough to get by. Quality pleases both God and man! How can our children become producers of quality work?

• *Activities that promote understanding of quality.* Ask questions at dinnertime like "What makes a quality car?" or "What makes a quality chocolate chip cookie?" or "What makes a quality book report?" You'll be surprised how their answers differ from yours. It is important that you and your children agree as to what constitutes quality.

• *Quality products.* Quality should be evident in the things we produce and buy. Think of the things you create, and look for quality workmanship. Why is it important? What happens when it isn't quality? How often do we return things we've purchased because of poor quality? Encourage your children to look for quality even in the things they themselves will purchase with that allowance they've been saving up.

• *Quality relationships.* Quality in relationships is reflected by not merely accepting family members or friends, but by being kind and doing good to others regardless of whether or not they are kind or good to you. This is a lifetime lesson. It requires constant encouragement.

• *Quality personal pursuits.* Whether or not your child is involved in soccer, scouts, piano lessons, or youth group at church, there are a few issues that promote quality in these areas: Finish what you start, do it with a happy spirit, do it with a humble spirit, do it to the best of your ability.

• *Quality academics.* Quality in your children's schoolwork is reflected by whether or not they do more than is expected. If you ask them to write five sentences about George Washington, they do quality when they write eight (assuming they're not just rambling without any concern for the contents). Remember, quality is doing more than expected. Only doing what is expected is average—a C! God expects more. Impress upon your children that the diligence they show now will gain them heavenly rewards.

Although we are sinners living in a fallen world, we desire perfection. But perfection can only be found in God. Our goal is to become as much like the Lord Jesus Christ as possible while we are here on earth. Everything we do should bring Him glory. And producing quality work brings glory to God. It may be difficult, but it is not impossible. Teach your children that the quest for quality is what matters most. "Be sure to do what you should, for then you will enjoy the personal satisfaction of having done your work well, and you won't need to compare yourself to anyone else" (Galatians 6:4, NLT).

AN EFFECTIVE COMMUNICATOR

Poor communication skills are blamed often during marriage counseling. Neighbors, friends, and family all suffer from the effects of faulty communication. Our society communicates in a multitude of ways, but are these communications effective? How can we teach children to communicate their thoughts, feelings, opinions, and criticisms clearly and effectively?

• *How do you know when you're communicating effectively?* Every speaker knows when he's lost his audience. He can hear it between the silences. How effectively you communicate can be measured by audience attention, audience participation, and whether or not your audience responds in action to your message. This is even true between two people. When you speak to your children, you know whether or not they are listening and are really hearing what you have to say. Many speakers mistakenly believe that what they have to say is most important. But what the listener needs to hear is more important.

• *Tone vs. content.* Our mothers have all told us to "watch your tone with me." Why? Because it communicates your real message. What you say may not be as important as how you say it. Your message can easily be drowned out by your tone. The content is important, but make sure your tone doesn't disguise it as something else.

• *Effective listening.* I used to tell my students they needed to use their listening behavior. Where should your eyes be? Where should your hands be? What should your mouth be doing? Effective listening is respectful listening, but it doesn't end there. Effective listening is active listening. Do you listen but in reality are just waiting for your turn to talk again? Active listening asks questions, makes comments, and acknowledges understanding. Are you an effective listener?

• *Understand your audience.* If your child is going to prepare a speech for a small group of homeschoolers at his local library, does it matter if his language is more appropriate for adults? Is your listener tired, annoyed, or confused? Have you even noticed? We must teach our children that they must first know and understand their audience before they speak. Similarly, they may write a letter to a friend and go on and on about how well they did in swimming this year, forgetting that their friend can't swim yet. We must help our children think outside themselves before they speak or write.

• *Written communication.* Some people believe that the art and skill of writing has fallen by the wayside due to the age of computers. I disagree. What you write represents who you are—even what you write online. What do we think when we get E-mail from someone and their message has a multitude of spelling errors? The *mechanics* of writing are just as important in conveying your message as the *art* of writing.

• *Oral communication.* Homeschoolers must look for opportunities for their children to present what they have learned orally. There are speech contests all over the country for just that purpose. Start early by hosting a "Come look and see what we learned this year" night. Invite friends and relatives over, serve food, and let your children describe in detail what they learned.

• *Creative expression.* We can also communicate who we are and what we believe in creative ways. Artists communicate via a variety of means. They may paint, draw, write, sculpt, dance, sing, act, etc. But your child doesn't have to be an artist to be creative. Maybe he has an original or unusual way of sending a card. My son makes a face in every letter he writes! Encourage creativity.

• *The art and skill of debate.* Debate is intimidating to many, and yet its value surpasses the trepidation it causes. Being able to effectively offer your opinion along with supportive evidence is a great skill. As Christians we will be called to do this over and over.

• *Socratic questioning.* This age-old method of exploring comprehension gives us the opportunity to ask all those why questions we were discouraged from asking when we were little. It causes us to dig deeper and think harder. It helps us draw our own conclusions and evaluate the opinions of others.

Christ is an effective communicator! His Word has been presented to us through all the means examined above. As we study the Bible we are made aware of tone, context, audience, questioning, etc. But these aspects of communication are not limited to the Word of God. They apply to everyday life with everyday people. They may not always ensure that your message will be received and heeded, but they will increase the odds in your favor. It is especially important that you, as parent and teacher, evaluate your own communication skills. Ask God to reveal your weaknesses in this area so you can more effectively communicate to your children all that God wants them to learn. "Let your conversation be gracious and effective so that you will have the right answer for everyone" (Colossians 4:6, NLT).

AN EFFICIENT RESEARCHER

We must know where to go to find needed information. The choices abound, but the time is still limited (maybe even more so). Learning to take the initiative to find the answer to a question, concern, or problem is necessary to succeed in this life. Even the basics of knowing who to call when you need help is a survival skill. Don't give your children all the answers. They will learn more by searching for themselves. The process is key. An efficient researcher can:

• *Locate and use several different types of resources.* Growing up, I thought this meant using more than one brand of encyclopedia! In this information age, one must be able to draw on a variety of sources for information. Books, periodicals, the Internet, CD-ROMs, videos, first-person interviews, and more are all ways to gain information. No report or project should rely on only one of these.

• *Keep accurate records of observations, readings, and interviews.* Even second graders can learn how to record what they've learned from their sources of information. After watching a video on lions, ask your child to write one thing he or she learned from it. Each source should have an accompanying reflection or paragraph about what was gained.

• *Gather and document data relevant to the selected topic.* Define your topic and then gather resources that are relevant to it. You may not use all the material, but it is always better to have too much than too little.

• *Utilize efficient note-taking skills.* Teach paraphrasing early! First graders can learn how to put things into their own words. Your child needs to be able to pick out topic sentences and create outlines, to learn how to write summaries and conclusions.

• *Draw conclusions; make predictions and personal application from collected data.* Now that all the information has been gathered, categorized, and summarized, what do you think about it? What is the bottom line? How will it help you or someone else in the future? How has it affected what you believe or what you do?

We will live in an information age for the foreseeable future. There will be more and more information to manage and explore. Children must learn how to find what they need when they need it. Look again at the competencies listed above. This is very similar to inductive study of the Bible. Each increases the breadth of understanding and encourages further growth. Each is a proven method of study. "Let all things be done decently and in order" (1 Corinthians 14:40, KJV).

A PROBLEM-SOLVER

So often we are reactive instead of proactive. We don't take the time to think or plan ahead. When trouble comes, we panic and let our emotions determine our actions. This is ineffective and sometimes even dangerous. Help children learn that a decision-making or problem-solving process takes the fear out of the situation and inserts logic instead. The process of problem-solving includes *understanding the difference between effective and ineffective decision-making.* An ineffective decision-maker or problem-solver is reactive. He flies by the seat of his pants. He allows his emotions to control his thinking and his actions. But an effective decision-maker or problem-solver is proactive. This person plans ahead for what he will do if something happens. This person chooses logic over emotion. Here are four steps to follow:

• *Define the problem.* Sometimes this is the hardest part. It is sometimes difficult to put our finger on what exactly is wrong, especially when we're upset. So write the whole mess down, calm down, and then try to see the real problem in the mess.

• *Evaluate possible solutions.* Brainstorm possible solutions or alternatives. List them, and judge them according to whether or not they are capable of solving your problem.

• *Develop a plan of action.* After choosing the most logical solution (not necessarily the one you like best), make a plan of action. Form a step-by-step method of implementing this solution.

• *Adjust plans when necessary.* Did your chosen solution work? If so, move on. If not, go back to your list of solutions, choose another, and try again.

Perhaps you've heard the popular saying, "God laughs when men make plans." And sometimes the opposite is true. Remember Abraham and Sarah? What did they do when God told them His plans? They laughed. Their son, the son of the promise, was named Isaac, meaning "laughter." If God is not included in your decision-making or problem-solving, it may not be your laughter you hear—it may be tears of anguish. God has provided us with the intellectual ability to make educated choices in this life. But our emotions are not reliable sources for decision-making. It's not what you *feel* that matters—it's what you know to be true.

> *People like that should not expect to receive anything from the Lord. They can't make up their minds. They waver back and forth in everything they do.*
>
> —JAMES 1:7-8, NLT

A CRITICAL THINKER

Discernment is probably one of the most important abilities we possess. However, it is tragically rare in today's world. Truth seems elusive and relative. It may seem dangerous to stand on the truth, but it is ultimately more dangerous to ignore it. Critical thinkers can:

• *Analyze problems and generate supportive arguments for both sides of a com-*

plex issue. Playing devil's advocate is one way to do this. Looking at each side of the issue objectively and providing an argument for it is another.

• *Utilize the scientific method.* This age-old method of gathering and analyzing information is quite effective. Don't skip it with your children.

• *Use deductive reasoning skills.* Drawing conclusions based upon what is known or seen is a basic reasoning skill. However, many of us are more expert at reading into things.

• *Support opinions or assumptions based upon available evidence.* "I think this because. . ." The *because* precedes your evidence. Never say "Just because."

• *Determine whether proposed reasons are reliable and/or relevant to the situation.* It is easy to get off the subject during heated debate. That usually indicates that emotions have overtaken the individual and logic has left the building. We must be able to tell if what is being said is relevant to the topic at hand.

What is the truth? In this world where truth is relative, it is crucial that our children know the truth as presented in the revealed Word of God and are able to see it clearly against the false ideas of this world. Discernment is not just a nice thing to have; it is necessary for our survival. It makes the difference between life and destruction. It cannot be overemphasized!

Sometimes we place too much value on our understanding of the information presented to us. The greatest challenge comes when we must measure what we have learned by the revealed truth in the Word of God. In a sense we do this according to the world's knowledge base. But more importantly, we must sift what we have learned through God's truth. Man's wisdom is not sufficient, but the Word of God is sufficient for all things. Keep God as the constant in your formula, and what you will be left with in the end will always be pure truth.

> *"Give me an understanding mind so that I can govern your people well and know the difference between right and wrong. For who by himself is able to govern this great nation of yours?"*
> —1 KINGS 3:9, NLT

We have considered target behaviors that demonstrate a person's mastery of various competencies. It should not be expected that children will exemplify all of them initially. They need to be encouraged and developed over time. Look at your curriculum, and see where you can offer your children opportunities to explore each. For example, keeping a journal helps children engage in self-reflection. Setting the timer when they do their math demonstrates time management skills. It is up to you set up situations for them to practice these skills. I caution you not to teach these skills in isolation. Many homeschoolers buy curriculum titled "Teaching Time Management" or "Teaching Critical Thinking Skills." If you've already done so, use them to teach yourself, but teach your children through everyday situations and circumstances. That is not only more relevant, but then there is one less workbook for your child to go through.

JUNETTA

This is what I wrote in 1988, regarding my philosophy of education:

I believe that our children are a heritage (gift) from God. They belong to Him and have been entrusted to us. For the time they are with us, we must prepare them to become godly men and women who will fulfill God's purposes for them and make an impact on the world in which we live.

I believe that we are responsible to our children to love them, to provide for them, to protect them, and to direct them. This is a privilege. I desire to raise them in the nurture and admonition of the Lord, to train them up to be mighty in spirit, and to have personal convictions based on the Word of God.

I believe that knowledge is good, but in training children, knowledge alone leads to pride. The information they learn needs to be added to the foundation of faith and virtue/character development (2 Peter 1:5-8).

We learn by example, by what we receive through our five senses (experientially through discovery), by what we read, by asking questions (and answering them), and through spiritual insight.

This is what I would add to it now:

As we are all different from one another, so are our learning styles. Variety and creativity in teaching styles is important to strengthen areas of weakness, as well as to produce a well-rounded child.

Seeing life applications of what is being learned is crucial to understanding and educational development.

I desire to strive for excellence with flexibility and to lead/encourage my children in doing the same.

Just because a book or a course is finished, doesn't mean I am. We must always continue to learn and grow. The proper use of what I learn leads to wisdom.

The early, loving discipline of a child produces a more respectful, content, and self-disciplined individual later. Teaching children that it is better to serve than to always be served helps them become team players.

Regarding socialization, I think it is preferable to have limited and controlled time with peers. The mass socialization we see in large school/class settings may equip our children with skills in pack-like behavior but is less successful at producing in them the vital interpersonal and communication skills that a warm and loving homeschool environment will. The low student-teacher ratio can greatly optimize positive socialization, academic education, and training in exemplary character.

FOR MORE INFORMATION ON THIS TOPIC

Success in School: Building on Biblical Principles by Vicki Caruana (Focus Publishing, Bemidji, Minnesota, 2000).

COUNT THE COST/REAP THE JOY

Take time now to explore each competency. Match strategies and curricula to each. How can you encourage them in your children?
Self-directed Learner

_____

_____

_____

Producer of Quality Work

_____

_____

_____

Effective Communicator

_____

_____

_____

Efficient Researcher

_____

_____

_____

Problem-solver

_____

_____

_____

Critical Thinker

_____

_____

_____

Do I Have to Do This Alone?

SOME PEOPLE WHO are considering homeschooling envision a parent and children sitting at the kitchen table together day in and day out without any contact with the outside world. That's why society always asks the socialization question first. There are indeed dangers in trying to do this thing called school by yourself. Some are more obvious than others. A balance must be struck between remaining isolated and becoming too busy outside your home. Homeschool co-ops and umbrella schools are two common ways homeschoolers interconnect. There are advantages and disadvantages to both. Your comfort level is probably somewhere in between.

THE DANGERS OF ISOLATION

Believe it or not, isolation is a choice we make. It doesn't just happen. In the beginning many homeschoolers are so consumed with managing their new lifestyle that time out of the house is considered detrimental. During my first year of homeschooling I fell victim to this very situation. I wanted to make sure I had everything under control; so I never attended a support group meeting, went on a field trip with others, or enrolled my children in additional classes of any kind. I politely said no to any invitation to meet with other homeschoolers, even for a day in the park. I was afraid that if I started going to activities outside my home, we would fall behind in our studies and would not be able to catch up. My insecurities made the decision to remain isolated for me.

Sometimes we choose isolation over participation because we are afraid that we or our children won't measure up. Sometimes we're too lazy to get outside the house. And sometimes we're too tired or overwhelmed to even reach out for help when we really need it. God did not intend for us to walk in this world alone. Are you spending all your time at that kitchen table? Can you find your way to step outside, even if just for one hour per week? Consider the natural consequences if you do not:

• *Decreased social interaction.* Many homeschool families are blessed with many children. They learn how to get along, how to share, how to tolerate, how to forgive, and how to bless each other on a daily basis. But some do not have large families; so it is important to expose children to a variety of social settings in which they can practice these skills.

• *Feelings of inadequacy.* It is very easy, alone in your home, to mistakenly believe that no one is going through life the way you are. It is also very easy to compare your child or yourself with other homeschoolers with whom you interact infrequently. Spending time on a regular basis with others brings us all down to the same level playing field. You'll begin to notice that you aren't the only one struggling. In fact you may find that you have something to offer someone else who is hurting more than you!

• *Increased stress.* Some personalities thrive on having their children around 24/7; however, there are just as many who require a time-out if they are to be effective when they need to be. Grabbing a nap or going out for coffee with a friend seem to be unattainable luxuries. Then there's the added stress of the guilt you feel for not just loving every minute with your children! Give yourself a break and sign your children up for a class or a park day with other children. And don't feel guilty!

• *Tunnel vision.* You can only go by what you know. If all you know is what you do, then everyone else will seem wrong to you. You will believe, falsely, that your way is best for every child in every situation. You become one of those homeschoolers who scare some people away from homeschooling and give others the ammunition they need to continue to criticize homeschooling. As a former teacher I had definite tunnel vision. I saw things one way, and it was the best way in my opinion. Then I began to meet homeschoolers and spend time with them and saw that there was more than one way to teach. If I had stayed in my own little world of teachers and traditional school, I wouldn't be here today, homeschooling my own children!

• *Decreased witness.* You've probably heard the advice, "Don't preach to the choir." As an isolated homeschooler, you're not even doing that. Actually, you're preaching to the preacher! How else will people, even those who criticize homeschooling, see what a blessing it is if you lock yourself away in your own home? Choose to be a visible force in your community!

Michele homeschools her four children ranging in age from five to eleven. It is only her third year of homeschooling, and yet she is on the verge of burnout. Her oldest needs more challenging work. Her second child has low self-esteem issues. Her third child had seizures until recently and experiences memory loss. And her baby, the kindergartner, has been diagnosed as ADHD by their pediatrician, who has recommended medication. Michele, at her wit's end, is strongly considering putting their children back into public school. She feels inadequate to meet their many needs. She is tired and doesn't see any other solution. Yet Michele hasn't really looked. She relies solely on her own abilities to homeschool. She believes, and rightly so, that the responsibility rests squarely on her shoulders.

Unfortunately, none of us is completely equipped to meet all the needs of our children. We have our own strengths and weaknesses as teachers. We have our own threshold of tolerance. God knows our limitations. After all, He made each of us, and He didn't make a mistake or forget anything. In Him we are complete, but only in Him. Relying on self leaves God out. He has provided a myriad of ways to help you meet your children's needs. Sometimes He uses other people.

THE UMBRELLA SCHOOL

An umbrella school is one that oversees the education of home-schooled students. Such schools exist either as private schools housed in actual buildings or as virtual schools. The services provided vary from school to school, but there are basic services that all provide. As you consider whether or not to register with an umbrella school, keep in mind your needs, your future in home-schooling, and the cost. Even if you have friends who register with a particular umbrella school, that doesn't mean you should. This is an individual decision, one that can be revisited every year.

Types of Umbrella Schools

When you register as a homeschooler, you usually have two choices in most states. You may register with the state through your local school district, or you can register with an umbrella school that is classified as a private school according to state statutes. Either way you are counted and are not expected to show up in a public school. Umbrella schools exist to meet the needs of those homeschoolers who desire accountability but do not wish to be accountable to the state alone.

Private schools. Some private schools offer an umbrella program to homeschoolers. This usually means that you will register with that school, and the school will in turn maintain records for your homeschool. Most umbrella private schools require that you follow the same curriculum the school does. For many families this is a relief. For others it is bondage. Advantages to choosing a private school for your umbrella school are:

• It may be the school you pulled your children from, and you like the curriculum.

• They will maintain and house all your homeschool records so you don't have to.

• Your child will be tested at that school every year.

• Many private schools allow you to enroll your child part-time for a fee.

Curriculum-based schools. Some curriculum publishers also provide umbrella schools. If you use only their curriculum, you may also choose to enroll in their umbrella school. They will maintain records of your child's achievement and progress. They will provide end-of-year testing. They will provide you with diagnostic feedback if your child is not progressing at the expected pace. You will have a complete academic report card for your child at the end of the year. Some companies require you to send all their work on a predetermined schedule to be graded and recorded. They take responsibility for all paperwork!

Support-group-based schools. Many homeschoolers want the security of an umbrella school without the obligation to teach what the school prescribes. Some local homeschool support groups have filled that need. They have registered themselves as a private school and are expected to fulfill state requirements as such; but there is usually much more flexibility for participating parents. Some of the services provided might be record keeping, curriculum discounts, yearly achievement testing, curriculum consultation, and even high school transcripts and commencement. Each group has its own membership requirements and accountability methods. There is also a fee attached to such services.

Long-distance academies. Some private schools that have been successful as homeschool umbrella schools have opened up their services up on a nationwide basis. You can register with them no matter where you live, but the same stipulations apply as previously described.

What They Can Do for You

Some of the services provided by an umbrella school include but are not limited to:

• Record keeping of grades, attendance, and achievement test scores.

• High school transcripts and commencement.

• Field trips.

• Curriculum discounts.

• Private school enrollment status.

Tuition and registration requirements will vary. Again it is important to talk to someone who is already enrolled and ask questions to find out if an umbrella school is advantageous to your family.

THE CO-OP EXPERIENCE

Co-ops are becoming the method of choice for homeschoolers to interact, provide meaningful learning experiences for their children, and get that sometimes much needed break! But not all co-ops are the same, varying not only in size and shape but in function and quality. Choosing to become involved in a co-op can be confusing, but for the most part the advantages outweigh the disadvantages. The challenge for many is to find a co-op nearby.

What Is a Co-op?

A cooperative, most commonly referred to as a co-op, for home-schoolers is an effort on the part of families to teach together. The size of a co-op may range from three to hundreds of families. The smaller the co-op, the more personal the interaction. For example, in a co-op that includes six families, a topic of study is taught by different parents alternately. That way one parent is responsible for every sixth week of teaching, while the others have a day off to themselves. This gives children the chance to sit under someone else's instruction and provides them with a wider circle of friends. Children in smaller co-ops may be taught together with all ages. Instruction usually occurs in the teaching parent's home. The challenge for the teaching parent in this instance is to teach to a variety of levels. The cost of such a small co-op is usually minimal, if there is any cost at all.

There are larger co-ops that may include tens to hundreds of families. These co-ops are usually held in a rented facility or a church building. They are highly organized and offer a wide variety of classes from which to choose. Offerings may include Spanish, state history, creative writing, biology, chemistry, Latin, band, or even sign language. The variety of choices is usually what attracts parents to larger co-ops. In such a large co-op children may be grouped by either age or grade, and there may be a limit on the number of students who can enroll. Teachers are homeschoolers who volunteer their time to teach a particular class. The price for a large co-op will be higher and therefore cost-prohibitive for many families. Keep in mind that you may be able to trade enrollment for volunteering either to teach a class or for other duties. Sometimes scholarships are available on a need basis.

How often a co-op meets also varies. Some meet once a week, while others attempt to offer two days of classes. How often you go may depend upon how much it interferes with your weekly schooling. Some co-ops may be far away, and you must consider travel time in your decision-making. It may not be worth driving an hour one way for a two hour co-op. But if the co-op offers your child something you cannot or do not feel equipped to teach, it may very well be worth both the drive and the price!

Why a Co-op?

A co-op makes sense for many reasons, but what is important is if it makes sense for you and your children. You know their needs, and you also know what you yourself can and cannot handle with regard to homeschooling. It is easy to get too involved in outside activities as a homeschooler. It is important to balance your activities with time at home together. Ask yourself first if you are comfortable with your children being taught by someone besides you. Are you prepared for the influences others may have on your child as they spend more time away from you? Do you need some time away for yourself? Does your child need something academically you do not feel prepared to give? Does your child shy away from interaction with others and therefore needs to branch out? All of these questions are involved with choosing to join a co-op.

Some co-ops offer classes for secondary students that may intimidate a parent. For example, if science is not your area of expertise and you have an older child, you may want to consider that biology lab offered at your co-op. Or if your child is very artistic and you wouldn't know watercolors from tempera paint, enroll her in the art class your co-op offers. The bottom line is: If it fills a need in both you and your child, it is worth taking the chance.

How to Choose

Small or large, formal or informal, in a home or at a church, academics or fun classes—the choices abound. Again the important thing is to know the needs of your child and then choose accordingly. If you are already involved in a number of outside activities, joining a co-op may not sound attractive right now. It becomes one more thing to fit into your already hectic schedule. But if you have yet to partake of anything out in your community, a co-op might be a good way to start.

One way to find out if a particular co-op is for you is to talk to someone who is a member. What were those parents' experiences like? What frustrated them or their children? What did they get out of it? Was it worth the drive or price? If you have a friend whose children are in that co-op and you want your children to spend time with them, it might be well worth joining. There are so many reasons to join. Just choose carefully.

Look at the classes offered. If you join, then you will lose a whole or at the very least half a day with your children. Will they be learning something you aren't comfortable teaching, to fill a gap? Or will they be learning something that is unrelated to what you want to teach, and you'll have to spend time catching up on "real" school when they come home? The only reason to enroll your child in a "fun" class is for socialization concerns. If it is your child's only opportunity to make friends, it may be worth it. Just don't punish yourself or your child for the time away, or you'll end up blaming the co-op.

Homeschooling does not have to be a lonely pursuit. In fact, it shouldn't be! The danger of burnout is high in individuals who try to go it alone. We build too many monsters in our heads, worrying if we are doing enough, long enough, and well enough. And when we're overwhelmed we have nowhere to turn if we've stood firmly alone. God did not make us to live in a bubble. He made us to serve Him, spread His Word, and bring Him glory using the gifts He's given us. You can't do that alone at your kitchen table. You can't work for the kingdom if you don't live in it.

JULIE

Why We Homeschool
1. We get to see our girls.
2. We can control what they learn.
3. We can interweave the Bible into education.
4. We can focus more on character building and training the heart.
5. We can teach life skills since the girls are with us more.
6. Teaching our children one on one is the optimum teaching method for learning.
7. It's enjoyable.
8. Their education becomes a family way of life.
9. It's less expensive.

FOR MORE INFORMATION ON THIS TOPIC

Family Matters: Why Homeschooling Makes Sense by David Guterson (Harcourt Brace, 1992).

COUNT THE COST/REAP THE JOY

If you still haven't found out about your local homeschool support group, now is the time! Ask other homeschoolers, check out your state online at www.hslda.org or ask the homeschool representative at your local school district office.

Attend one meeting, even if it is just to find out about co-ops or umbrella schools in your area. Practice those efficient research skills, and find the answers to your questions about umbrella schools and co-ops.

What questions do you still have?

1.

_____

_____

_____

2.

_____

_____

_____

3.

_____

_____

_____

4.

_____

_____

_____

5.

_____

_____

_____

6.

_____

_____

_____

Home-School Partnerships

I NOW PRESENT TO you a radical statement: Homeschooling is not for every child. Nor is it for every child in every family at all times. Since that is true, others will inevitably become involved in your child's education. Partnerships between home-schoolers and their traditional counterparts do exist and are on the increase as more and more educators realize the potential of homeschooling, and as homeschoolers realize the answer to prayer many teachers are in their children's lives. These partnerships have many faces and forms. But first the bridges must be built so that they can exist at all.

WHAT DO THESE PARTNERSHIPS LOOK LIKE?

Chris has dual-enrolled in his neighborhood public elementary school so he can attend the gifted program there one day per week. Anna also dual-enrolled at her elementary school so she can take art and music there. Justin has dual-enrolled at his local high school and takes biology and biology lab each day. Debra has finished her high school requirements at age sixteen and attends the local community college part-time. Whether in sports, special education, art, music, band, or community college classes, homeschooled students have the opportunity to expand their horizons.

What benefit do public or private schools gain from partnering with homeschoolers? In such an image-conscious society, it is in a school's best interest to form these partnerships. Homeschooling is a mainstream movement, and to be against it is becoming increasingly unpopular. Word of mouth is the fastest and most effective way to spread both good and bad news within the home-school community. If a public school is welcoming homeschoolers, everyone hears about it. Conversely, if a school does *not* welcome homeschoolers, everyone will hear about that as well. Another benefit to schools is money. Even if a child only attends a public school part-time, he is counted, and federal or state money is then allocated for him. Therefore the school receives more money because a homeschooler has chosen to attend, even if for only one hour per week. That's better than not at all. And for educators whose only goal in this life is to teach children, they are intrigued by the chance to work with homeschoolers. These are children they might not otherwise see. Yet this partnership is not as easy as it seems or as beneficial as one might hope. It takes both sides to ensure a successful experience.

How Can These Partnerships Be Cultivated?

Joan walked into the local elementary school with hesitance. Was this a good idea? Would her daughter benefit from being here for just one class? Would the school even be receptive to the idea? Joan hadn't stepped foot into a public school since she herself graduated twenty years earlier. Yet the fear that always accompanies going to the principal's office was uncomfortably fresh! After twenty minutes of waiting in the outer office, Joan approached the secretary's desk like a timid kindergartner.

"Oh, you're still here," the secretary said. "I'm sorry, I thought I told you—Mr. Knight just doesn't have time to figure this out today. He's never had a request like yours, and frankly he isn't comfortable granting it."

Joan thanked the secretary and turned to leave. But before she did she said, "I've heard wonderful things about the music program at this school. We just thought maybe it would be a good place to learn from the best."

The secretary wondered if this parent would ever return. She hated being the bearer of bad news. She wrote down the name so she'd remember it just in case things did change.

This scenario is common, but unfortunately not as common as one that includes a confrontational and demanding homeschool parent. The "I pay taxes, don't I?" routine does not build bridges. It just creates walls. In order for you to build relationships with your neighborhood school, you must first be visible. Attend community events sponsored by the school. Go to the annual book fair. Go to the science fair. Go to the football games, concerts, and awards ceremonies. These are not closed events. Introduce yourself to the principal and teachers at these events. If you enjoyed it, praise them for a job well done.

If there is a school advisory committee whose members include people from the community, volunteer to be on it. If your school has never worked alongside homeschoolers before, this kind of groundwork is necessary. If you are fortunate enough to have a school that has already welcomed homeschoolers, make sure you strengthen that bridge and not weaken it with your interaction. Then when it is time to actually attend a class or program offered at that school, it should be an easier step than expected. Schools' goals include serving their communities. This is one way they can do that.

WORKING FOR A QUALITY EDUCATION FOR ALL CHILDREN

The greatest threat to a budding partnership is the "us against them" mentality. We see ourselves on separate sides of the equation when in actuality we are all parts of the solution. Public and private school programs and classes are all part of the alternatives we can choose and use to reach the target for our children. If the goal is to provide a quality education for our children, we must be open to utilizing different strategies and taking different paths than we initially thought necessary. But just as homeschooling is not for every child, neither is partnering with public schools for every child. I urge you to know the needs of your child and then to choose appropriately.

There are myths and misconceptions on both sides. Many teachers think homeschoolers are unqualified and misguided. Many homeschoolers believe the same about teachers! It is not necessarily your job to actively dispel these myths about homeschooling, but you should never be a part of perpetuating them. If you refuse to be counted in a survey or don't complete required paperwork with your state or go to school board meetings with a list of demands, you've done nothing to promote goodwill and nothing to put homeschooling in a positive light. Just as a Christian must consider whether how he lives attracts others to Christ or repels them, the homeschooler must consider how he comes across to the world around him. I know it's easy to say, "I don't care what others think about what we do! It's up to them to accept it." Yet as a Christian I encourage you to be a light for homeschooling. And the best way to do that is to build those bridges.

STAYING INVOLVED ONCE YOUR CHILDREN ARE GROWN

A dear friend finished homeschooling her youngest child, then sent her off to college. Bess let out a much deserved sigh of relief. There were so many things she had said no to while homeschooling. Her children always took priority. But now she had time for herself and for others. During her first year on her own she spent more time attending Bible studies and building herself up spiritually. She sought God and His will for her now that her children were gone. By the end of that first year, however, her next step was obvious. Many new families in her church had recently made the decision to homeschool. Many more came to her for advice since she had homeschooled longer than anyone they knew. She was considered a sage, a woman of wisdom. Bess found herself counseling and consoling, and these families found her considerate and captivating. A new ministry was born; but more importantly Bess found herself walking within God's will for her. Titus 2 exhorts the older women to

> *train the younger women to love their husbands and their children, to live wisely and be pure, to take care of their homes, to do good, and to be submissive to their husbands. Then they will not bring shame on the word of God.*
>
> —TITUS 2:4-5, NLT

What a privilege it is to guide young homeschool parents! What an honor to be working to build up fellow believers in this way! You don't have to look far to find your place. It's somewhere familiar; it's somewhere close by. You may have finished well with your own homeschooling experience, but the race is not yet over. If you've been given the gift of teaching, use it to the fullest. Look for opportunities to teach in your church, your community, even in your public or private school. After your turn at homeschooling is done, you can still help build and strengthen the bridges.

 ZAN

One afternoon, as my then ten-year-old daughter and I were frantically preparing a project for a homeschooling program called the Masters Academy of Fine Arts, we discovered the family motto (for my side of the family) on the family coat-of-arms: *Rien Sans Dieu*. Translated, this French phrase means "Nothing without God." This one phrase encapsulates my view of life and education—they are nothing without God.

This affects my choices for my children in many ways. We have chosen mainly Christian texts (both traditional and nontraditional—KONOS, Greenleaf Press) for one reason: As the children read, I want them to read from a Christian perspective. They are certainly inundated with the secular on a daily basis through media, peers, and jobs as they get older, so I do not worry about them being isolated. Of course, we read the classics and discuss world- and life-views. We discuss other philosophies of life and creation and critique them in light of Scripture.

We dialogue a lot, all the time. How does Scripture impact the study of math? As Christians how do we view the situation in Bosnia? What can we learn from history that can positively impact our lives as citizens today? How can we serve our neighbors and those around us in need? How can our gifts be used in furthering God's kingdom and choosing a career? Why are good manners important, and why is it wrong to be rude? Every subject and every lesson spawns a new conversation. And such conversation is the bedrock of the education I am giving my children. The curriculum I choose is a tool—like an artist choosing a paintbrush. The final product is the well-rounded, thoughtful child, not a completed work-text.

In preparing for their high school years, I already knew their strengths and weaknesses, their personalities and their passions. Ty is an athlete, a people person, and a gifted communicator. John, while a gifted athlete himself, is a scholar and a lover of math and science. Ty will find his niche in politics or sales or the ministry. John wants to be an oral surgeon, which will give him the freedom, as he sees it, to be active in ministry, politics, and his family life.

I chose a college-prep track for both of them in high school. I taught many things—history, English, economics, government, literature. (I used a combination of Bob Jones, A Beka, KONOS, the Internet, real books, and travel.) For math, we chose the Chalk Dust video series. For all of their lab sciences, they attended a weekly four-hour lecture/lab taught by a gifted, retired teacher who is committed to the inerrancy of Scripture. For Spanish I, II, and III, I hired a tutor. In these classes outside the home I was able to choose adults who excelled in their fields and could serve as role models in terms of their faith.

As Ty grew older, we found ways for him to exercise his gifts—serving as a Senate page in both the South Carolina and United States Senates. He attended Boys State and worked with TeenPact. John did all these things as well, but was also able to do some unique things in the area of science, beginning at age fourteen with a medical missions trip to Mexico where he actually pulled teeth, gave injections, administered sutures, and surgically removed teeth. Both boys have traveled overseas for combination study and missions trips.

Their *work* in the real world at the State House, etc., and their *service* in the real world—tutoring in inner-city projects, missions trips, and car-ing for the elderly and handicapped—kept their Christianity from being sterile and merely academic.

They have had abundant lives and have experienced real interactions in both the community, the church, and the world at large. They love Christ and want to serve Him. The world has truly been their classroom.

COUNT THE COST/REAP THE JOY

Partnerships are also characterized by written agreements. Make sure you know what is expected of both sides. Dual-enrollment is becoming quite popular. Don't let the "enrollment" part scare you. For accountability and insurance purposes you must formally enroll your child at his or her school.

1. What programs or classes would be worth investigating at your local school?

_____

_____

_____

2. Who is your contact person at the district office?

_____

_____

_____

_____

3. Are there deadlines and space availability issues?

_____

_____

_____

_____

4. What concerns do you foresee with such an arrangement?

_____

_____

_____

5. What benefits do you foresee with such an arrangement?

_____

_____

_____

Index

Notes

Notes

Notes

Notes

Notes

Notes